DIGITAL CHINA:

WORKING WITH BLOGGERS, INFLUENCERS AND KOLS

Rave Reviews

"Nowhere more than China, no time more than now, working with influencers isn't just important, it's critical. It sits at the convergence of the biggest trends of our times: commerce, technology, social media and trust. But with so many options and such intense competition, you need a guide. You're holding it now. Page by page, chapter by chapter, the opportunities and options will become clear. This book will open your eyes, save you time and map out a shortcut over a mountain of challenges and possibilities. You've found it."

— **Andy Crestodina, Co-founder and Chief Marketing Officer of Orbit Media Studios and author of Content Chemistry**

"For any business executive looking to sell to Chinese consumers, Dudarenok and Hallanan's book is perhaps the best guide that provides key insights on how companies can utilize China's army of KOLs to build brand awareness and generate sales. Giving detailed examples, this book should be read by all executives trying to understand the changing e-commerce landscape in China. I highly recommend it!"

— **Shaun Rein, Founder of China Market Research Group and author of The War for China's Wallet: Profiting from the New World Order**

"Ashley Dudarenok, both in person and in writing, is energetic, thoughtful and an influencer in her own right on the topic of Chinese social media and marketing. She and co-author Lauren Hallanan deliver great insights on KOLs, with unique observations on their role as intermediaries between brands and consumers and thoughts about their future. All brand managers serious about China should get their hands on this."

— **Erwan Rambourg - Managing Director at HSBC and author of The Bling Dynasty, Why the Reign of Chinese Luxury Shoppers has Only Just Begun**

"Wow! As a marketer in the West, I've been more than intimidated by the size and cultural differences in the Chinese market. That is, until Dudarenok and Hallanan's book! This book has opened up all sorts of new possibilities for me and my clients and given so much insight. I recommend anyone thinking of expanding their audience into Asia to read Digital China. It's sure to become a well dog-eared reference on the desk of many Western marketers."
— **Tara Hunt, CEO and Partner at Truly Strategic and author of The Whuffie Factor**

"From WeChat and Weibo to Douyin (Tik Tok) and Yizhibo, Ashley Galina Dudarenok not only gives an insightful look inside the world of social media in China, she dissects it and reveals how to master it with Key Opinion Leader marketing campaigns. This book is a must-read for any business or marketing professional looking for a blueprint that will increase brand awareness, drive e-commerce traffic and win in China. "
— **Kelly Ann Collins, CEO of Vult Lab Social Media Agency, former USA Today journalist and one of the United States' first influencers**

"In China, even more so than other countries, influencer marketing is a critical channel to engage local consumers. Digital China provides an insightful overview of the key factors brands should be aware of before they develop a China influencer marketing strategy."
— **Joel Backaler, Global Marketing Strategist and author of Digital Influence: Unleash the Power of Influencer Marketing to Accelerate Your Global Business**

"China has taken the message of personal branding to heart, and has developed a powerful influencer market that's well worth understanding. This insightful book will show you opinion leadership, China style. In the early days of digital marketing, China learned from the U.S. Today, it's important for globally savvy marketers to learn from China."
— **Dorie Clark, adjunct professor, Duke University Fuqua School of Business and author, Entrepreneurial You and Stand Out**

To all those awesome marketers who work with Chinese KOLs.

This book is for you.

CONTENTS

CHAPTER 1

What Are KOLs and Why Do You Need Them?

A KOL is a key opinion leader. In the West, they're called influencers or thought leaders. They can be bloggers, online personalities or internet celebrities. Working with KOLs on Chinese social media is not just a necessity for businesses entering the market but also a key component in the marketing strategy of some of the world's most famous brands.

Influencers have a stronger influence in China than they do in the West. They have follower bases who see their opinions and suggestions as credible and influential but they don't just spread information. They also promote attitudes and approaches that affect the buying decisions of their followers and readers. Many also excel in driving online sales and unlike bloggers in some other regions, it's not unusual for them to engage in direct sales.

With the expansion of official WeChat* accounts and with the growth of new platforms, their followers continue to grow, increasing their influence and value.

Who are these KOLs? How do they operate? And why do Chinese consumers look to them so consistently? Let's find out.

*Note that WeChat has 2 versions - one for China and one for international markets. Access and functions are different for each. WeChat in this book refers to the Chinese version of the app which is called Weixin in China.

1.1 Who are KOLs?

To start off, it's important to clearly define what it means to be an influencer. A large following doesn't necessarily make someone a thought leader. A true influencer is someone who provides value related to their area of expertise and builds a relationship with their audience over time. People trust them and turn to them for advice. For someone who has a large audience, but is more of a general entertainer, a more accurate title would be internet celebrity, or wanghong in Chinese.

Some Background

Chinese social media began in the late 90s with Tianya Club and Netease Blog. The bloggers on these platforms slowly evolved into the influencer scene that China has today.

Tianya Club (天涯社区) and Netease Blog (网易博客)

Tianya Club, founded on February 14th, 1999, was one of the most popular internet forums in China. It was a bulletin board system (BBS), an online forum that was used before the internet as we know it today, offering blog, microblog and photo album services. NetEase Blog came online in 2006. It was one of the best blog service providers and had 90 million users in 2010. People could write articles, blog or publish photos there.

Most Tianya users were highly educated and it was famous for its high-quality, user-written articles. It had influential channels, such as Tianya Zatan (天涯杂谈), which was an important source in journalistic and academic circles. It also provided a platform for first generation KOLs such as screenwriter Cai Shen Ning (宁财神).

However, Tianya also provided a platform for people like Shi Hengxia, known as Sister Furong (芙蓉姐姐), a self-promotional, self-involved and self-delusional young woman who was in many ways a prototype for online personalities to come, both inside and outside China. She posted videos and photos of herself in her signature S-shaped pose wearing tight-fitting, low-cut clothing that often left little to the imagination. Her arrogant, titillating and controversial statements triggered thousands of discussions.

In 2013, Tianya Club still had 85 million users, but after Weibo came out, people gradually abandoned it and NetEase's blog closes on November 30th, 2018.

After these two early examples, others achieved followings online for various reasons. Actress and director Xu Jinglei (徐静蕾) started a blog on sina.com in October 2005. Instead of dealing out juicy gossip from the film world, she concentrated mostly on day-to-day happenings, her TV watching habits and updates on her cats. By July, 2007, her blog had the most incoming links of any blog on the internet and had more than 100 million page views. She also published a book of her blogged articles. Writer Han Han, a best-selling author who blogged about current affairs, politics and car racing was also very popular around this time. He hit a nerve with his controversial positions on touchy topics and took Xu's crown about a year later with around 210 million hits on his blog to her 209 million.

With the birth of Weibo came new ways to reach mass internet audiences and a new crop of influencers. Yao Chen, an actress who came to fame on a popular TV series in 2005, quickly gained an audience on Weibo and now has more than 80 million followers. She's known for shining a light on issues related to refugees, pollution and censorship and in 2013, was the UNHCR's first goodwill ambassador in China.

Papi Jiang started posting original short videos on Miaopai in 2015 and went viral on Weibo in 2016 when her videos got more than 290 million views on major media platforms in just four months. Her trademark jump edits and accelerated video speed allowed her to deliver social commentary and comedy in a high-pitched voice and won over viewers. After gaining fame, she engaged in some high profile ad campaigns and has received funding from investors. Her use of swear words also earned her the attention of regulators who temporarily took her videos offline until required edits were made. She currently has more than 28 million followers on Weibo.

Other platforms also began to create their own stars. Douban, a site for book, music, movie and television reviews produced Nan Sheng. From the post-90s generation, she gained fame for posting beautiful photos of herself in traditional costumes and stylings from different eras. She eventually became a working actress in 2012 and a published author in 2013.

Douyu (a live streaming site that, is different from Douyin) is similar to Twitch and features live-streamers playing video games or performing for their online audience. Douyu personalities are referred to as hosts or anchors. Feng Timo, another young woman from the post-90s generation, became an anchor in 2014 and gained a following based on her live singing broadcasts. Although she started out singing cover versions of famous songs, she now records and releases her own songs and has appeared on TV variety shows. She has 13.8 million fans on Douyu and 8.4 million on Weibo.

Li Ge, known as Kelly in English, is a young woman who was one of the first to go viral on Douyin, known as Tik Tok outside of China,* one of the most recent entries to China's online mobile landscape. Li is known for doing cute, entertaining dances to popular songs and for her singing videos. Known as the leading lady of Douyin, she has over 43 million fans there and just over 1 million on Weibo.

*See the Appendix for a list of platforms and some prominent bloggers discussed in this book.

The Situation Today

So while influencers have existed in China for some time, the idea that someone could make money by growing a following on the internet didn't become mainstream until the emergence of stars like Papi Jiang (Weibo: papi酱) and WeChat and Weibo influencers like Gogoboi (Weibo: gogoboi) and Becky Li (WeChat: Miss_shopping_li). As a growing number of brands started working with influencers, Chinese consumers started understanding the earning power of social media.

The tipping point occurred when live streaming exploded in China in late 2015. What was different about live streaming was that anyone could do it and live streamers could monetize their fan base right away through virtual gifting. The internet was filled with stories of streamers earning hundreds of thousands of yuan* a month.

*yuan = RMB, renminbi, "the people's currency", China's currency

And there are cultural and economic factors at play as well. The average entry level salary for college graduates is very low and competition is fierce. It can take years to slowly rise through the ranks and earn a decent wage. On top of that, the best jobs are in major cities, leaving fewer career options for those in lower tier cities and rural areas. There's always been a lot of family pressure to get a stable, high paying job and, as consumerism has grown, this pressure has increased.

Now, being an internet celebrity is an aspiration among China's youth just as young people elsewhere want to become famous Youtubers or Instagram influencers. For many, becoming "internet famous" seems like a good get-rich-quick plan, as well as a way to avoid the boredom of a traditional job. However, unlike true opinion leaders, these internet entrepreneurs are typically focused on growing large audiences as fast as possible by any means. Their strategy is self-focused and motivated by desires for money and fame rather than a genuine desire to serve their audience.

One of the consequences of this explosion in popularity of both online platforms and KOLs in general has been increased scrutiny from China's internet regulators. As a result, they implemented China's New Advertising Law in September 2015. It restricts the use of celebrity endorsements and regulates the marketing of pharmaceuticals, medical equipment and health food. Promoting products and services commercially, without clearly stating it's an advertisement, can now potentially get you into trouble, and forwarding content deemed false or harmful can result in liability. Because of this, and greater demands for transparency and authenticity from online fans, brands and KOLs are identifying sponsored content more clearly than in the past.

The Five Main Types of Internet Personalities

1 Wanghong

These are a type of internet celebrity that brands should generally avoid. They're usually defined by the following characteristics:

- They often become famous because of their good looks and charming personalities, not because of any particular knowledge or skill.

- Wanghong may have large followings and be very popular, but their audience is usually very broad.

- They aren't seen as a trusted resource on any particular topic and typically hold little influence over their audience in this regard.

- They often grow rapidly due to viral content so their audience hasn't known them long enough to trust them.

- Wanghong have little staying power. Their fame can be fleeting as their followers get bored of them quickly and move on to the newest flavor of the week.

Collaborating with wanghong may seem successful as their posts and live streams may get very high view numbers, but because they aren't true opinion leaders, it's unlikely to generate meaningful results for your brand. There's nothing to be gained by partnering with an online personality who has a large audience but little actual influence.

2 Next-generation Content Creators

A step up from wanghong, these are talented creatives who love to produce high-quality, entertaining content, but still have no particular area of expertise. They often have loads of loyal fans, but their fans aren't following them to learn about new products or watch tutorials. They want to be entertained, not learn, get advice or shop.

This type of content creator is especially prevalent on short video platforms such as Douyin. Working with them may be helpful for generating broadly aimed brand awareness but isn't a great way to reach a niche target audience or generate sales.

3 Key Opinion Leaders

Unlike wanghong, who see the growth of the influencer economy as a way to get rich, key opinion leaders see social media as a platform to share their expertise and develop a personal brand. They're more strategic with their choice of platforms and content style and are focused on serving their audience, sharing their knowledge and building a community.

4 Celebrities

This includes famous actors, singers and TV personalities. They have large fan bases and unprecedented name recognition. They've also got well-established images. People are keen to imitate them and many are experienced in terms of doing promotional activities. As a result, these influencers do not come cheap.

5 We Media

These are smaller media companies, often run by former or current journalists. They often appear to be a single individual yet there may be multiple people writing on a niche topic. They tend to post on current affairs and social issues as well as other topics of general interest.

1.2   The Characteristics of High-quality KOLs

So, how can you tell if you're dealing with a true KOL? How can you separate the influential from the merely mediocre? Let's find out. Here are 7 characteristics of high-quality KOLs.

1 They're laser-focused on a specific topic

KOLs have an area of expertise that they're passionate about and the majority of their content centers on this topic. They probably won't work with brands that are unrelated to their area of focus.

2 They usually have professional experience or training related to their chosen topic

For example, many top KOLs are former journalists, photographers and makeup artists. This gives them the confidence and ability to create high-quality content. This also means that many of them have authority and strong connections within certain industries or academic areas.

3 They have a distinct voice and content style

Top KOLs know it's important to create a unique personal brand that resonates with their core audience. KOLs who stay neutral, follow trends or try to be everything to everyone aren't as influential as those who have a clearly defined persona. This is becoming increasingly important as China's Gen Z consumers, those born from 2000-2009, who are called post-00s, have shown how much they value individuality and personal expression.

4 They're community leaders who strive to provide value to their audience with the content they create

A KOL's relationship with their fans is the key ingredient to their success. Their posts can get four times as many views and eight times as many interactions as a luxury brands' own posts because of their fans' support.* They spend a great deal of time on content development but they also spend a lot of time interacting with their followers. Answering as many fan comments and messages as possible is part of being a KOL and many spend several hours a day responding to comments and managing their follower communities.

*See the Bibliography for a full list of sources and references.

5 They're strategic and have a plan for the development of their personal brand

Influencers are very careful about the platforms they use and the type of content they produce. KOLs are adept at evolving and pivoting to include new platforms and styles of content as the online market changes. However, unlike wanghong, who hop from platform to platform trying to make a buck, influencers maintain long term accounts on multiple platforms to reach a wider audience and mitigate risk. As their following grows, they often hire a support team and, instead of relying entirely on brand sponsorships for income, many launch their own brands.

6 They've developed their audience gradually

KOLs are not in a rush to make clickbait content and grow a massive audience overnight. Instead, they consistently provide value and build a relationship with their audience over time. They know that focusing on steady, long-term growth will give them a loyal, trusting audience.

7 They value their reputation more than money

Influencers are very selective about which brands they work with. They don't want to alienate fans or tarnish their reputation. They know that doing too many sponsored posts and posts about products that aren't in alignment with their personal brand will cause a backlash and they may lose followers. True opinion leaders turn down money rather than risk hurting their image.

1.3   China-specific Influencer Trends

> *"Mega-influencers like Chiara Ferragni and Kylie Jenner might be magnetic on Instagram, but China's most powerful KOLs (key opinion leaders) are new-wave media magnates. Constructing multifaceted empires across China's diversely developed digital scene, they run their brands with flourishing features and compelling storytelling on Weibo (Chinese Twitter), WeChat (the most versatile chat app in the world) and Tik Tok (China's Snapchat)."*
>
> — Vogue UK, August 31, 2018

The Professional Turned KOL

With the advent of social media, it became very common for professionals to start publishing content independently and building their personal brand. Prime examples are internet experts and fashion editors and stylists who no longer need their magazines to reach an audience. Both relish the chance to communicate with the public directly through their own social media, sharing their experiences, thoughts and ideas. This is also true for makeup artists and stylists who are now able to share their expertise and give advice to the masses. Many of China's top beauty and fashion thought leaders spent many years grinding away, honing their skills before beginning to publish content on social media. Li Kai Fu and Leaf Greener are two prime examples of this trend.

Li Kai Fu was educated in the United States and graduated from Columbia University and Carnegie Mellon. He has worked in top positions at Microsoft and Google and is one of the most popular bloggers in China with 50 million followers. His blog focuses on the topics of technology, achievement and education.

Leaf Greener is a former editor at Elle China who became an online influencer with her LEAF WeChat account. She has worked with Karl Lagerfeld, David Burton, LVMH and Lane Crawford and people follow her account for style and fashion tips and trends.

If you're lucky enough to encounter influencers who are at this level, it's best to refer to them by their professional title as many of them are highly qualified experts in their profession who just happen to have a large social media following. They're in a separate category from online personalities who trade on their popularity or entertainment value alone. For example, Leaf Greener is first and foremost a fashion editor, not a fashion KOL.

Social E-commerce Integration

In China, social media and e-commerce are completely integrated.

In other words, social platforms have e-commerce functions and e-commerce platforms have social functions. WeChat integrates with e-commerce mini programs. Weibo links to e-commerce sites Taobao and Tmall and even new short video platform Douyin has the ability to link to Alibaba sites. Then there are the e-commerce platforms. JD.com has live streaming and Taobao and Tmall have live streaming as well as their own social product recommendation platform Weitao. On top of that, there are platforms such as Xiaohongshu which blur the line between entertainment site, social network and e-commerce outlet.

This integration means that, in China, it's much more common for KOLs to directly promote products and for consumers to seek out KOL recommendations when purchasing products. This doesn't mean that influencers can create spammy content that merely pushes products and doesn't provide value to consumers. It just means that there's a more open attitude towards consuming content about products and in some cases it means KOLs are able to directly drive traffic to product listings.

KOL Brands

Although many influencers rely on the traditional sponsored post monetization model, in China, KOLs are increasingly following the model pioneered and perfected by figures such as the Olsen Twins, Jessica Simpson, Jessica Alba and the Kardashian family. They're creating their own successful brands by manufacturing and selling their own products specifically created for their audience.

Originally, this phenomenon existed primarily among Weibo influencers who built massive audiences for the purpose of driving traffic to their Taobao stores. Weibo was ideal for this since it's an open platform designed to spread messages to large audiences. The Weibo Window feature allowed followers to click product links in posts and directly purchase items from an influencer's Taobao store without ever leaving Weibo.

The advent of mobile e-commerce live streaming in 2016 provided a whole new opportunity for these influencers. They used Taobao Live and Weibo's live streaming platform Yizhibo as another tool to share their current merchandise through live, interactive fashion shows. The next phase in the KOL brand e-commerce evolution is seeing influencers opening their own WeChat mini program online stores to directly sell their own products or a curated collection of products from other brands.

1.4   Why KOLs Are So Important in China

"We're like a bridge between brands and users. KOLs make it easier for brands to find their target users, build connections with them and deliver concepts. The more consistent the brand and KOL are, the more overlapping the audience coverage is, the more valuable the marketing relationship is."

— Becky Li, Highly Influential Fashion WeChat and
Weibo Blogger

To understand why influencer marketing is essential in China, it's important to first understand the Chinese consumer.

1 China is not a single market

China is a large country with lots of regional diversity. Just as you wouldn't approach a customer in rural Texas the same way you would someone living in Los Angeles, you need to approach consumers in different parts of China differently. Each group has different needs and experiences different trends. A one-size-fits-all marketing campaign simply won't work and it can be extremely time consuming to create custom campaigns for each sub-market.

Collaborating with KOLs lets brands reach their target audiences quickly and easily. Developing audiences in each sub-market is more cost and time efficient through collaboration with influencers who already have an established relationship with them.

2 Young consumers pay little attention to mass media and traditional advertising

Chinese consumers are increasingly numb to old media advertising and have turned their attention to social media, influencers and niche online communities. By 2017, The China Research Center found that Baidu, China's Google, has already surpassed CCTV, the national broadcaster, to become the largest advertiser in China. This trend isn't about to reverse any time soon. If anything, trends indicate that things will become even more niche. It's easier than ever for people to find others who share their interests and within these online communities, influencers, thought leaders and experts will continue to emerge.

3 Savvy shoppers are overwhelmed with choice

There's a common misconception among western brands that China needs their product. Actually, Chinese consumers are overwhelmed with choice and these days it's extremely difficult to stand out. There was a time when there were limited options. Western brands stood out and may have been valued for that reason. Although some niches still benefit from increased trust in foreign brands over local ones, for many product areas, those days are long gone.

Chinese consumers have access to a wide variety of international brands and the number of domestic brands has also exploded in the past decade. Marketing approaches for local brands are sophisticated and many enjoy strong loyalty. Given this situation, consumers have a great deal of choice.

4 Consumers are afraid of making the wrong choice

Convincing a Chinese consumer to try a new product or brand is not always easy. Besides the fact that they're inundated with new product ads on a daily basis, there are some other things they're concerned about as well.

Safety is a big issue. There have been numerous product quality scandals in China which have caused consumers to be wary of anything new and unproven. For high-end products and travel, people want their purchases to demonstrate their style and taste and want to be able to show them off on social media. It doesn't need to be flashy, but if they're not sure of the quality, they may be reluctant to buy it. Fakes and low quality products are an issue and it's also difficult to return items in China. Dealing with customer service is a hassle and for cross-border purchases, refunds and replacements are often impossible.

5 Brand authority is crucial

For all these reasons, brand authority is crucial for Chinese consumers and they will scrutinize a brand's reputation thoroughly when a product piques their interest.

While product reviews and search engine results all play a role, influencers are a key component for building brand authority in China. When a well-respected influencer posts about a product, they're essentially putting their hard-earned reputation on the line and lending their authority and credibility to that brand.

6 Exhaustive research prior to purchase, particularly for big ticket items

Customers might be interested in a product but aren't in buying mode when they come across it the first time. People need to see a product several times before they take action. According to a study by McKinsey, this is particularly true for Chinese luxury shoppers, who need to come into contact with a brand or product seven to eight times before they decide to buy, as opposed to a standard American consumer, who only needs to do so about four times.

Influencer content is one of those touchpoints and is a key component of their research. A 2018 study by marketing consulting firm Westwin found that for Chinese consumers looking for foreign products, e-commerce platforms, search engines and KOLs are their main research channels.

7 Chinese consumers rely heavily on word of mouth recommendations

Word of mouth is important, especially for cross-border e-commerce. A mid-2018 report from Azoya Consulting found that 50% of cross-border consumers are influenced by in-person and online reviews, 32% take into account social media content and 25% are influenced by search engine results.

Although they've probably never met in person and are reading it online, consumers often value advice from their favorite influencers just as much as advice from close friends. In fact, the Westwin study mentioned above also found that KOL recommendations were the most influential purchasing factor with a whopping 67% of Chinese cross-border consumers claiming their purchases are influenced by KOLs. The rate was even higher for consumers between 25-34 years of age, at 75%. KOL recommendations were more important than product discounts (65%) and e-commerce platform recommendations (58%).

Because consumers rely so heavily on word of mouth, entire platforms are built around it. For example, Xiaohongshu, one of China's fastest growing social media platforms, is a community of over 100 million Chinese consumers who share product reviews for everything from makeup and skincare to travel and fitness. The site is a trusted resource for knowledge-hungry female consumers in particular. Alibaba, the creator of China's most popular e-commerce platforms, Taobao and Tmall, also knows the importance of KOL recommendations. It's investing heavily in its live streaming platform, Taobao Live, and Taobao and Tmall's social commerce platform Weitao (微淘) where KOLs and brands can post reviews and product-related content, build an audience and engage with platform users.

If you've made it this far, you now have a solid understanding of the present state of China's influencer marketing economy. As we go on, and you learn more of the ins and outs, just remember that there's no one-size-fits-all KOL marketing strategy. Each brand needs to craft their own distinct strategy based on key factors including their industry, budget, level of brand awareness, e-commerce strategy and desire for risk and experimentation.

CHAPTER 2

KOLs in Action: Revealing Case Studies

The advent of live streaming in 2015 was a key turning point for KOLs in China. Another breakthrough for KOLs occurred in 2017. Singles' Day on November 11th, or 11.11, is a big online shopping day in China. On Singles' Day that year, for the first time, China influencer brands broke into the top ten in terms of sales and four of them made over 100 million RMB (14.4 million USD) in sales.

Among these top selling fashion influencers were Anna (Weibo: onlyanna), Cherie (Weibo: 雪梨Cherie) and Zhang Dayi (Weibo: 张大奕eve), who's considered the most business-savvy influencer in China. Her store reportedly pulled in $46 million US in 2016, slightly surpassing Kim Kardashian's annual earnings of $45.5 million US.

This also showed that for high level influencers, their brands have the potential to disrupt the sales results of traditional retailers.

Now that we understand the state of the KOL industry, let's take a look at other ways these dynamics are playing out in real life. The examples in this chapter showcase the kind of impact and results KOL involvement can achieve. They show what large brands can do with great strategy, planning and big budgets, what can be achieved by nimble, resourceful, small brands and what KOLs are doing all by themselves. There are also telling examples of what NOT to do.

2.1   WeChat

Mini Programs Powering KOL E-commerce

A growing number of Chinese KOLs have launched their own brands specifically created for their audience. In the past, the majority of these brands were created by Weibo KOLs running their stores on Taobao because Weibo and Alibaba's partnership allowed a seamless buying experience.

However, as soon as WeChat launched its mini programs in early 2017, WeChat influencers jumped at the opportunity to launch their own brands as well. With e-commerce mini programs, WeChat influencers were finally able to integrate custom shops into their accounts.

Over the past year and a half, numerous top-tier WeChat influencers have launched brands.

The first big WeChat KOL to do so was Gogoboi, who launched his mini program boutique, Bu Da Jing Xuan (不大精选), in April, 2017. Rather than manufacturing his own products, he sells a curated selection of goods from luxury e-commerce retailers like Yoox, Net-A-Porter and Farfetch and partners with brands to launch their products exclusively on his platform. His most successful launch was Givenchy's Duetto bag, which sold out within 72 hours.

In December 2017, fashion KOL Becky Li launched her own mini program store (黎贝卡的异想世界) selling a line of products she created based on data collected from her millions of followers.

Then, on June 26, 2018 Chinese influencer Tao Liang, better known as

Mr. Bags, launched his WeChat mini program Baoshop, selling a jointly-designed, limited-edition micro backpack from TOD's. This marked the first time a luxury brand has premiered a product globally through a mini program created by and for a fashion blogger. The three hundred pieces available were priced at 10,800 RMB (1,500 USD) each and sold out in minutes. The bags were limited to one per person and there was a surprise bonus gift for the first 20 customers.

Many influencers who have their own brands still continue to collaborate and create content with outside brands, but established players have to be keep an eye on them as it's now easier than ever for these KOLs to transform into competitors.

Mid-tier influencers are also finding success. A prime example is fashion and lifestyle account sugarandspice (Wechat ID: sugar__spice), run by two Chinese women, going by the pen names Sugar and Spice, who curate fashion items from overseas brands for their customers. Some of the top selling items in their store include shoes and bags from brands such as Paul Andrew, Victoria Beckham, The Row, Proenza Schouler and others, hair care products from Christophe Robin, uka and Bamford, scented candles from Tom Dixon, Cire Trudon, Diptyque and Neom and other lifestyle and beauty products from overseas brands.

As a clue to how the e-commerce ecosystem is expanding along with new social media features, Beijing startup LOOK specializes in setting up mini program stores for brands and helped sugarandspice launch their store in early 2018. In 15 days, they made it into the Top 50 mini stores on WeChat.

2.2   Live Streaming

JD Live: Two Million RMB (288,000 USD) in Two Hours

Antoine Bunel, a widely recognized public figure and top food and beverage (F&B) KOL in China, is no stranger to e-commerce live streaming. With his enthusiastic stage presence and passion, Antoine is often invited to live stream for international brands on JD Live and Taobao Live, promoting everything from kitchenware and appliances to food products.

In early 2018, Antoine, who is originally from France, had the opportunity to direct and host a live stream to launch a French milk powder brand on JD Live. The two-hour stream garnered 10 million views and sold over 2 million RMB (288,000 USD) worth of product.

The keys to the promotion's success were threefold. Firstly, the brand worked with an experienced, professional KOL and gave him creative freedom. The brand knew that Antoine had much more experience with live streaming in China than they did so they handed over the reins, allowing him to direct the show. Next, they hosted the stream on an e-commerce live streaming platform. These include platforms like JD Live and Taobao Live. Hosting the stream on other more entertainment-focused platforms, such as Yizhibo, Huajiao or Inke, may have brought a lot of exposure but wouldn't drive sales. Finally, they partnered with an e-commerce platform. It certainly costs more but partnering with an e-commerce platform means that they'll promote it and drive targeted traffic to the stream.

> "Remember a KOL is a passionate, creative person who communicates enthusiasm to others. If you make a product a favourite in their arsenal, they're more likely to happily push it! I've given a couple of brands millions of impressions for free this way."
>
> — Antoine Bunel, Top F&B influencer in China

Taobao Live: ShopShops

Liyia Wu has built an entire business around leveraging Taobao Live to market and sell foreign brands. Her company, ShopShops, is a platform dedicated to connecting brick and mortar stores in the United States with consumers in China. They did this primarily through live streaming on Taobao and now do it through their own app as well.

Her massive team of nearly 80 live streamers (many part-time) are based in cities all across the US in cities such as Los Angeles, San Francisco, New York and Miami. Currently they host anywhere between 1-3 live streams per day and have done hundreds of streams since their initial launch in 2015.

ShopShops has worked with a variety of brands, including Phillip Lim, Opening Ceremony, Everlane, Anna Sui and Spanx. According to Wu, ShopShops garners an average of $6,000 US in sales per store event.

While this may not seem like a KOL marketing case study, much of ShopShops' success lies in the relationship that their viewers have developed with the channel's live streamers. As one journalist put it, "Watching the ShopShops' team at work is a little like seeing what your cool best friend discovered during an off-the-beaten-path shopping trip." Essentially when brands work with ShopShops, they're tapping into Wu's small army of micro-influencers.

In an interview for the China Influencer Marketing Podcast, Wu shared stories of the intimate relationships many of the hosts have with the audience, from sharing their bra sizes, to watching one host hunt down her car after it had been towed, customers feel like the streamers are their friends, not someone trying to force them to buy something. These relationships create trust between the audience and the streamer, which is why viewers are willing to purchase expensive luxury products online from someone they've never met.

2.3   Xiaohongshu

Campaigns on Xiaohongshu Should Be Discreet

Finding a good case study on Xiaohongshu isn't easy. That's because brand promotion on Xiaohongshu is different from other platforms.

Xiaohongshu is a lifestyle-sharing community which encourages users to generate content. Word of mouth marketing from authentic reviews is the platform's biggest strength. The more obvious the advertisement, the less-likely readers will trust the content and take action.

Although celebrities like Fan Bingbing and Lin Yun Jelly have accounts on the app and the products they feature see dramatic sales increases, most brands need to focus on smaller influencers and product seeding. On Xiaohongshu, campaigns that don't look like campaigns are the best campaigns.

Give free samples and invite bloggers on the app to write a product review post. In addition to free products, some smaller brands also pay influencers a nominal fee of 200-500 RMB (28-72 USD) per post.

While Xiaohongshu is becoming increasingly strict about sponsored posts and asks users to clearly state if a post is sponsored or if the product has been provided to them for free, it usually doesn't flag posts as long as they're objective, discuss both pros and cons and mention other brands and products.

Skincare tool brand The Beautools has been known to work with Xiaohongshu micro-influencers with less than 10,000 followers and searching for the brand yields over 2,000 results for their products. Yet, from a regular consumer's perspective, it's not noticeable as the brand has been consistently recommended by celebrities and large KOLs across a variety of social media platforms. While some of these posts may be sponsored, many are just from regular users sharing their experiences.

In mid-2018 facial masks by the Chinese brand RAY and foundation powder by Giorgio Armani have become some of the most popular items on Xiaohongshu. Is this due to a campaign on Xiaohongshu? Is it the side effect of a campaign on another platform? Or is it merely word of mouth? It's hard to tell. And that's the point.

2.4   Douyin

The breakout star of 2018 was short video platform Douyin. While everyone is eager to take advantage of the platform's massive popularity, some brands have seen more success than others.

O2O Challenges:

Douyin challenges are issued by a post stating or showing the challenge along with the related hashtag. Users make and tag videos with the hashtag for fun and entertainment and to compete for the top spot among the challenge videos. Brands have tapped into this and have issued some very successful challenges on the app.

Haidilao

The hot pot chain that got huge publicity for its viral Douyin video is none other than China's famous Haidilao whose viral Douyin campaign is an excellent example of how to use Douyin Challenges. Challenges invite users to compete to be the most popular video response to a request from an author. To get a challenge going, brands usually collaborate with influencers who create their own challenge videos which motivate their followers to do the same.

For the challenge, Douyin users had to go to a Haidilao restaurant to create videos showing how they made their unique hot pot. As of writing, over 40,000 people have participated in the challenge with combined views in excess of 50 million. What's most impressive about this challenge is that it not only generated massive online exposure, but it also drove offline sales as users had to go to the restaurant in order to film their video.

Answer Tea Owes its Success to Viral Douyin Videos

Answer Tea launched in January 2018 and viral videos on Douyin spurred 250 franchise requests across China.

What was so special about the videos? Answer Tea's drinks have a special packaging design. Customers can place their orders along with a question asking anything, from "When will I get a girlfriend?" to "Am I beautiful?" Opening the lid revealed a funny answer, making buying a drink there like using a sassy magic eight ball.

A video of a user revealing a humorous answer took off and soon everyone wanted to try it out for themselves, leading to thousands of user-generated videos and of course, a huge boost in sales. Again, one of the reasons this campaign was so successful was the connection it created between online and offline, requiring users to purchase products in order to film their own video.

What's important to note is that Haidilao and Answer Tea were able to drive sales because their products are relatively inexpensive. This strategy is unlikely to work for goods at a higher price point. Mid-range and luxury brands should expect little more than awareness from Douyin campaigns.

2.5 KOL Cautionary Tales

KOLs are not magical sales unicorns. Not every campaign involving influencers succeeds. They're just harder to find out about as brands and influencers are keen to sweep them under the rug. Here are some less than stellar examples that showcase essential mistakes that brands should avoid.

During the relaunch campaign of Dior's iconic saddle bag in mid-2018, one of their campaign videos, featuring Hong Kong fashion influencer Elle Lee, sparked a social media backlash. Chinese netizens mocked the unimaginative video saying that it dragged down the bag's cult status.

The brand didn't pay close enough attention to their choice of KOL, who many saw as not prestigious enough for the brand, didn't put enough effort into her styling and didn't create a compelling narrative for the video, which showed her in a very simple outfit in a Dior store merely looking at the bag and trying it on.

And it's not just foreign businesses that miss the mark from time to time. Chinese cosmetics brand Pechoin also misfired on a big campaign. It cooperated with WeChat KOLs to post an extended image with a nostalgic design. The total views from all the posts added up to more than 30 million. Unfortunately, the conversion rate only was only 0.00008. Part of the reason for the failure was their selection of KOLs. Most of them were known for popular creative content so their posts were widely circulated but not to people who were the brand's target audience.

"It's extremely important to understand influencers, what they've done and achieved in the past and why they're a great fit for the brand. On the other hand, it's important that the influencer understands what you want to achieve. This is key to realizing the best possible return on investment."

— Fabian Bern,
Founder and Managing Director of Uplab

Even Papi Jiang has been involved with campaigns that failed to flourish. She was featured in an ad for Swiss watchmaker Jaeger-LeCoultre. Although a well-known internet personality with a fair bit of fame offline, many felt her image didn't match the luxury brand. She's known as a funny, sassy girl next door who's not afraid to tackle social issues and swear, not as a fashion icon who flaunts status symbols. As a result, many didn't warm to the campaign and it became known more for the online discussion it sparked.

Brands need to be selective and only work with trusted KOLs that are a truly a good fit. This may take more initial research, but it will pay off in the long term. Furthermore, it's best to give KOLs the creative freedom to produce content that they know will appeal to their audience. The softer the sell and the more authentic and compelling the content is, the better the reaction will be.

CHAPTER 3

The Most Influential KOL Platforms and How They Work

WeChat and Weibo are China's biggest social media players. The average person in China spends a good part of each day on these platforms and they're the key online spaces that businesses need to reckon with. They occupy positions similar to Facebook and Instagram. Now imagine that you can pay for your groceries and buy intercity train tickets through Facebook and that Instagram and Amazon are linked so that you can buy promoted items with just a few clicks. That's social media in China.

But in addition to the big two, there are plenty of smaller, influential platforms that focus on different topics and fan bases. Choosing the correct platforms to market on also means keeping in mind what you want to achieve. Are you looking to improve brand awareness? Do you want to boost sales? Are you trying to build a client and fan database? Different apps, KOLs and formats suit each purpose.

Let's take a closer look.

The Big Two - WeChat and Weibo

3.1   WeChat

Overview

Tencent's WeChat, called Weixin in China, started as a free instant messaging app and grew from there adding more and more functions. The international version has more limited capabilities but the China version can be used to do everything from hailing a taxi to paying for international flights. Because it's inserted into the fabric of life in China and can be used to do so many things, users rely on it heavily. Over half of users spend more than 90 minutes on it every day and it's used for work by 90% of users.

Stats and Demographics

- Monthly active users: 1.058 billion (by Q2 2018 up 9.9% from previous year)

- Number of users that log in to WeChat every day: 902 million (as of Sept 2017)

- Number of official accounts: 20 million

- Monthly active official accounts: 3.5 million (year-on-year growth of 14%, as of Sept 2017)

- Monthly active users of official accounts: 797 million (year-on-year growth of 19%, as of Sept 2017)

As of 2017, over 40% of WeChat users were between 26 and 35 years old and more than three fourths of WeChat users were 18 to 50 years old.

Key Features

Moments

The Moments page is a semi-closed sharing page for text, images, short videos, articles and external links. All the posts can only be seen by a user's WeChat contacts. According to a report from the China Internet Network Information Center, as of June 2018, 86.9% of WeChat accounts use the Moments page. Brands can grow followers on their official account through content shared by users.

Official Accounts

Anyone can sign up easily for a personal account to use WeChat's messaging functions and follow official accounts. For an official account, a registration process is required. There are three types of official account - subscription, service and enterprise - that are equivalent to a basic account, a business account and a corporate intranet account. An official account is required in order to market and advertise effectively on WeChat. They provide a channel for famous people, government, media and enterprises to connect with millions of WeChat users. General users can subscribe to official accounts established by brands, media and individuals. These accounts publish articles that cover news, product reviews and more. Most update daily or weekly so people get a lot of information through official account subscriptions.

Mini Programs

Mini programs are cloud-based embedded apps within WeChat. Brands and KOLs can leverage mini programs to nurture a virtual community, launch creative campaigns, build an e-commerce platform and even promote their brick-and-mortar stores.

KOL Cooperation Formats

Advertorials / Product Placement / Embedded Marketing

Native advertising and embedded marketing are the most common ways for brands to work with WeChat KOLs. They write an original, informative article about a topic in their usual style that features the product or uses images featuring the product in the article.

For a sales campaign, brands can ask KOLs to insert a sales link at the end of the article. Tracking codes in the purchase links distributed to different KOLs can help measure their effectiveness and calculate the final commission based on a PPS (pay per sale) pricing model.

Product Reviews

For brands, this is the most straightforward way to introduce their products and services. Many WeChat KOLs are experts in their field and regularly write informative, reliable product reviews and product comparisons. These are often paired with giveaway campaigns or links to the product's online sales page. Brands that partner with WeChat KOLs who genuinely like their products can reach a large audience and see a noticeable uptick in sales.

Sponsored Campaigns

Brands sponsoring KOLs to launch campaigns is another common practice. KOLs introduce the campaign and offer gifts sponsored by the brand. They can also direct traffic to the brand's official account by integrating the brand's official account QR code at the end of their articles.

Co-branding or KOL Cross-promotion

Sometimes, brands co-create a product with a KOL and sell it as a limited edition. A great example of this is the co-branding between Mr. Bags and Givenchy at the beginning of 2017. 80 limited edition bags worth 1.2 million RMB (173,000 USD) were sold out in 12 minutes. After this successful campaign, Mr. Bags did similar co-branding ventures with other luxury brands like Burberry, Tod's and Chloe.

Sales on KOLs' WeChat Stores

More and more fashion KOLs have their own WeChat stores or mini programs for e-commerce purposes. Brands can offer special editions of their products in the KOL's WeChat stores.

Ads and KOL Promotion

With their high exposure, WeChat ads can help maximize the effect of KOL promotions, making their articles more visible to as many potential users as possible and it's advisable to run KOL promotions and complementary ads at the same time.

Moments Ads

Moments ads look like normal posts and users can interact with them by liking them or commenting but they have a "Sponsored" tag in the upper right corner. They can be used to promote an official account or a campaign, encourage users to download an app, distribute coupons and launch location-based promotions. WeChat users check their Moments updates frequently so investing in these ads greatly increases exposure. Advertisers can define their target users according to their gender, age, location, industry, marital status, education level and more.

Account Ads

There are three major types of account ads. They are footer ads, video ads and exchange ads. They can promote an official account or a campaign, encourage users to download an app or distribute coupons. Brands can also advertise products in their WeChat Store and can enable users to purchase the item by clicking the ad.

Mini Program Ads

These ads are displayed as a banner on a mini program page. The mini program admin can decide whether to place it on the top, in the middle or at the bottom of the page. They're similar to footer ads in format and can be used for campaign or e-commerce promotion.

Case Study

In mid-January 2018, on their 190th anniversary, French perfume and cosmetics brand Guerlain launched a campaign on Chinese social media with the theme of "Beauty and Evolution". Top Chinese actress Fan Bingbing was their brand representative.

Guerlain, understanding that many Chinese consumers follow expert KOLs on the platform who strongly influence their purchase decisions, cooperated with some top cosmetics KOLs on WeChat like Meiya (美芽, WeChat: meiyaapp) and IAMINRED口红控 (WeChat: IAMIN-RED) in order to reach potential customers.

In their promotion articles, both KOLs talked about new brand representative Fan Bingbing and wrote product reviews for the brand's new lipstick. At the end of the articles, they had calls-to-action to purchase the lipstick on Guerlain's official website and provided a promotional code to win an additional small gift offered on a first-come-first-served basis. IAMINRED口红控 also launched a giveaway campaign, encouraging readers to comment to win an exclusive edition of the promoted lipstick.

The campaign was a big success. Many readers commented under the IAMINRED口红控 article and most of them spoke highly of the lipstick and the colour. In total, both articles exceeded 50,000 views and sales on Guerlain's official website doubled compared with the previous year.

3.2 Weibo

Overview

Officially launched in 2009, Sina Weibo is the leading microblogging and social networking site in China and another must for marketers. "Weibo" is the Chinese word for "microblog". Since Sina Weibo is the most popular microblog, when people say "Weibo" they're referring to Sina Weibo.

Weibo is an open platform for microblogging and social networking. It was developed for users to follow celebrities and share user generated content (UGC). Weibo is the most dominant source of news and gossip and people are there mainly to stay up to date, share and comment. But more than this, the huge popularity of short videos and live streaming have played a major role in Weibo's popularity and it partners with video sharing app Miaopai and live streaming app Yizhibo which users can access through Weibo.

Stats and Demographics

- Monthly active users: 431 million (by Q2 2018, year-on-year increase of 70 million)

- Usage rate among the Chinese public: 42.1% (up 1.2% from the end of 2017)

- 93% of monthly active users access Weibo via mobile devices

- Over 50% of Weibo users come from third and fourth tier cities. 16.2% are in first-tier cities and 26.2% are in second-tier cities.

- Over 80% of monthly active users on Weibo are below 30. Young adults from 23 to 30 make up 38.4% of MAU (December 2017)

- 56.3% of users are male and 43.7% are female.

Key Features

Users can make their own posts and interact with other people's posts by liking, commenting and reposting. In January 2016, the 140 Chinese character limit, which already allowed much more content and meaning per post than a 140 characters in English, was removed for original posts. Users can make longer posts although readers won't see all of the text in their feeds. Posts can also include images, videos, music, emoticons and polls without needing plugins. The 140 character limit still applies to comments and reposts however.

KOL Cooperation Formats

Sponsored Posts

These are like traditional paid media ads, except the content is created by the KOL and written in their voice. All you have to do is provide them with a content outline and other material related to your product, services or campaign. It currently seems that any links to e-commerce sites other than Alibaba properties are blocked.

Product Reviews

These are best if your KOL is an expert in a certain field.

Campaign Launches

The most common type of campaigns for KOL cooperation are giveaway campaigns. They usually require users to follow the account, forward a designated post and/or tag friends for a chance to win gifts.

Social Selling

This is getting more popular among Chinese KOLs. New rules on Weibo require e-commerce links to Alibaba properties only and penalize posts that mention firms specializing in sales, marketing or advertising. Payments are usually on a commission basis. The more clicks or sales they can generate, the higher their commission.

Live Streaming

These feature a thought leader interacting with your brand or your product and can include links for viewers to purchase the item or get a discount. Payment is usually on a commission basis based on the number of clicks.

Ads and KOL Promotion

Ads must be used in conjunction with a KOL strategy on Weibo. It's not an option. It's a necessity to reach an audience on this open, active, fast-changing platform. Compared to WeChat, Weibo offers more diverse and targeted advertising options for brands to increase exposure and reach out to focused market demographics.

The four major advertising options are display ads, Weibo search engine promotion, fan headlines and fan tunnel. It's important for brands to tailor a strategy for each type of ad and a combined approach often works best.

Given the open nature of Weibo, launching ads hugely boosts post exposure and is a good option to increase the reach of influencer posts. Fan headlines and fan tunnel are the best tools for this.

Display Ads

Also known as banner ads, they're featured on Weibo's homepage, on the search page of the Discover section, and on the side of users' news feeds. Advertisers can choose various sizes and placements for desktop and mobile versions. They can also select keywords to control their visibility based on user searches and have them displayed on relevant accounts. These ads are usually for promoting events, sales or other campaigns.

Weibo Search Promotion

This is a great way to increase the visibility of your account and bring traffic to your page. Weibo has a native search engine so users can search for accounts and discussions based on keywords. This promotion format puts your account at the top of the list for particular keywords. The price depends on the popularity and competitiveness of the keywords you choose.

Fan Headlines / Fanstop

This type of ad is useful for boosting posts to existing followers to increase exposure and enhance engagement. Boosted posts appear once at the top of their news feed if they refresh the page within 24 hours. The boosted post looks like a regular post except it has a "promoted" tag. The price for each promotion depends on the number of current followers; the more followers you have, the more expensive it is. It's the most common way for KOLs to boost their posts so that their followers will see their post immediately when they open Weibo.

Fan Tunnel / Fensitong

These ads reach out to a target audience and are a good way to increase followers. You can define the target audience by age, gender, region, interests and even device types. At the same time, you can also target followers of other accounts with similar niches. With this type of ad, users that aren't your account followers are still likely to see your boosted posts.

Case Study

The calcium supplement brand Caltrate launched a promotion campaign on Weibo to boost sales at their Tmall store on International Women's Day, 2018. Their target audience was women in their thirties who have to deal with the pressures of daily life and the signs of aging.

Right before Women's Day, Caltrate produced an impressive video, depicting the challenges middle-aged women face. The video successfully hit the pain points of many female consumers and struck a chord with them. The supplement brand also created the hashtag #Women with a backbone are confident# (#骨气女人有底气#) to encourage users to voice their opinions.

Caltrate cooperated with several top female bloggers, including Su Qin (Weibo: 苏芩), Nuanxiaotuan (Weibo: 暖小团), Xiuxianlu (Weibo: 休闲璐), and well-known female volleyball player Hui Ruoqi (Weibo:元气少女惠Rachel) to make a short video. They posted it with the topic hashtag and encouraged women to repost and comment. The Weibo campaign was a success. The topic hashtag accumulated over 66 million views in a short time.

Other Major Players

"Don't just go after the "Big KOL". Make sure there's a mix of micro-KOLs, traditional paid media, O2O and experiential marketing in every campaign."

— Jeff Fish, Co-founder of TMG Worldwide

3.3   Xiaohongshu

Overview

Founded in 2013, Xiaohongshu (小红书) is an information sharing community and social e-commerce app that focuses on cosmetics, fashion and lifestyle products from outside of China. As such, it's also a cross-border e-commerce hub. It offers a glimpse into the lives of contemporary, young, middle-class and affluent consumers. As of June, 2018, it had about 100 million registered users and 30 million monthly active users from around the world sharing their lifestyle tips on the app. In 2016, with the help of big data and machine learning technology, it began targeting users with specific content. The app's homepage algorithm serves content to users based on what content they've liked in the past, what they've searched for and their behaviour on the site. This has helped make it a favourite with users and a valuable site in terms of influencer marketing. In 2017, its sales volume exceeded 6.5 billion RMB (937 million USD).

Xiaohongshu started as a shopping tips community and that community is now its unique calling card. It's a trusted site where users go to get word of mouth recommendations from Xiaohongshu's huge database of reviews and comments and also has an e-commerce component.

User Demographics

The app's user base is young and confident with lots of personality. "Be yourself" is their motto and self-disclosure is their essence.

Women between 18 and 35 make up 70% of users and the app is increasingly popular with the post-95 audience. Users mostly buy mid-range and high-end products and the site attracts users looking for quality and uniqueness.

The Xiaohongshu Douyin Connection

Xiaohongshu is frequently used as a product research tool. Consumers often learn about a product or brand from a campaign on another platform and then hop over to Xiaohongshu to learn more about it and read user reviews.

This happens most frequently with products and brands featured on short video platform Douyin (Tik Tok, formerly musical.ly). Because videos are only 15 to 60 seconds long and focused on entertainment, viewers can't get much detail about the products they see. So, after seeing a product on Douyin, people often search for the term Douyin + the type of product on Xiaohongshu.

Entering the Chinese characters for Douyin (抖音) into the Xiaohongshu search bar brings up over 40,000 results as well as numerous product combinations. Since Douyin is a primary platform for food and fast moving consumer goods, combinations such as such as Douyin spray, Douyin chicken feet, Douyin cake and Douyin gifts are not unusual.

As just one example, a sunscreen stick from Korean brand JM Solution became very popular on Douyin in mid-2018. At the same time, the number of posts about it on Xiaohongshu also increased to over 15,600.

KOL Promotion

> *"The the game on Xiaohongshu is different. It's very content driven. If your product and content are good, then people will find you."*
>
> — Elaine Wong, Founder, Double V Consulting

Prominent celebrities, such as actresses Fan Bingbing and Lin Yun, are on the app but it hasn't changed the original atmosphere of equality and community. As more and more celebrities transform themselves into beauty bloggers and lifestyle gurus, the more important apps like Xiaohongshu become and the more popular products recommended by influencers become.

The community is a "super opinion group" composed of many small influencers each with their own character and appeal. When KOLs are trusted and liked by the community, the products they recommend can go viral. It's also a good platform for product seeding.

When brands choose KOLs on Xiaohongshu, not only should they match the brand's image but they also need a distinct personality. To find the right KOLs to cooperate with, brands can use KOL databases and agencies.

*See the Appendix for a list of well-known agencies.

- The app's posts are called notes. They include text and pictures. Users introduce a brand or product and share their experiences. Purchase links can also be attached. A smart move by brands is to send KOLs products and ask them to write reviews, user guides or recommendations.

3.4   Douyin / Tik Tok

Overview

Short video is one of the most popular social media formats and Douyin , which is called Tik Tok outside of China, is the most promising platform for them. Launched in September 2016, Douyin is like former app Vine - a short music video community aimed at young people that focuses on music, fashion and style.

In 2017, Douyin blew up following a partnership with The Rap of China, an extremely popular reality show centered on rap competition. The app went from 17.4 million daily active users in December, 2017 to more than 150 million daily active users as of June, 2018 and became Apple's top downloaded app in the first half of 2018.

Douyin's interface is simple and intuitive, as users only need to click three times to like a video and swipe to switch content. 15-second videos are also perfect for mobile users and creators as they can be made and watched on the fly. Clips can be edited easily with special effects such as "repeat", "flash" and "slow shot".

Content is shown to viewers based on their interests, hobbies, age and viewing history. Douyin also features hashtags which are often used to prompt platform-wide challenges. Brands can use this feature to issue challenges with incentives or prizes for the best challenge entries. This helps gather user-generated content, spreads brand awareness and increases engagement.

User Demographics

As of June 2018, Douyin had 300 million monthly active users and 150 million daily active users in China and 500 million global monthly active users. 66% of its users are female while 34% are male. Users under 24 years old account for 75.5% of users while 25-30-year-olds account for 17.5%. About 45.3% of users come from 1st and 2nd tier cities.

In terms of income, half of them earn 3,000-8,000 RMB (432-1,150 USD) per month, and 14.7% of them earn more than 8,000 RMB (1,150 USD) per month. Douyin has more educated users than other short video platforms like Kuaishou and 41.9% of them hold bachelor's degrees.

KOL Promotion

There are five main categories of content that are popular. When brands leverage KOLs to enlarge their influence and exposure, working with these content types is the easiest way to grab audience attention.

"We've run the numbers on previous campaigns and found that the product category with the biggest opportunity to both 'go viral' and convert sales on Douyin is food and beverage. To date, hot pot chains, bubble tea franchises and snack foods have been some of the biggest beneficiaries of Douyin's stratospheric rise. There's a strong focus on entertainment and instant gratification"

— Michael Norris,
Consumer Research Manager at Resonance China

Challenges

Brands can cooperate with KOLs to launch a challenge and to encourage their followers to take part in a campaign. For example, Michael Kors invited three well-known fashion KOLs to shoot videos with its new items and stickers to launch its City Catwalk Challenge. Total views for the videos exceeded 5 million.

Stickers

Brands make logo graphics that users call stickers to display in the corner of videos to encourage KOL imitation by the audience. For example, Secoo launched a campaign with a sticker of its box logo and the slogan "Giving you the best things from around the world." KOLs Da Chuan (Wiebo: 元气大川a) and Hui Hui Zhou (Weibo: 慧慧杨) shot initial videos with the logos displayed and appealed to fans to participate. More than 114,000 users engaged in the campaign.

Live Streaming

Brands can cooperate with KOLs to do live streaming. During the broadcast, KOLs can demonstrate products, share links recommending products and share purchase links.

Novel Skills and Techniques

Some KOLs, called "技术流" (Jishu Liu), use unusual skills to get attention. These kinds of videos easily garner attention and start trends. This type of content suits car brands as well as electronics, online games and trendy new products.

Music and Dancing

These fall into a few types. Some KOLs specialize in their own original music. Brands can commission a song related to their brand. These can be very effective for campaigns that want to present a strong and clear brand image or to strike a chord with the audience. The second type involve performances choreographed to songs. This kind of content is good at conveying energy and emotion and encouraging user engagement. The third type involves KOLs who are talented at lip-syncing popular songs.

Fun, easy, creative dances are popular on the app as people can follow along with them and participate easily. Car brands, electronics, fast fashion and games fit well with this kind of collaboration.

3.5   Kuaishou

Overview

Kuaishou was launched in 2011 as "GIF Kuaishou" to make and share GIFs. In 2013, it changed to a short video sharing community and by May 2018, it claimed it had 120 million daily active users who spent an average of one hour a day on the app.

Kuaishou's content is known for being diverse, lowbrow entertainment and much of it is in the style of prank and dare shows in the West. It's a bit like Reddit as popularity is decided by the user-community. There's plenty of stunting, eating, singing, anecdotes, crude jokes and "Let's Play" style videos, where people broadcast themselves playing computer games.

As such its content has also been subject to scrutiny by China's State Administration of Press, Publication, Radio, Film and Television which asked it to remove content it called "vulgar" and "harmful" in April 2018. It was banned from letting new users register until further notice. Hundreds of videos were deleted, some accounts were blocked, and it changed it's AI, which promotes videos popular with viewers, to diminish the influence of this type of content.

Kuaishou's interface is quite simple. Users see video feeds ranked by the system's AI, which also takes into account a user's preferences and viewing history. They often see different content each time they open the app as new content enters the system and popularity shifts. The main attraction of the app is that it doesn't seem to be dominated by big names, celebrities and known influencers. Instead, users feel a sense that anyone from within the community whose content becomes popular can make a name for themselves. Kuaishou's business model is built on commission fees on gifts and rewards sent to users and revenue from ads on the site.

User Demographics

First and foremost, Kuaishou targets young audiences in 3rd and 4th tier cities and the countryside with a down-to-earth style popular in these areas. This niche is unique as most social media platforms ignore this demographic.

Kuaishou users include high school students, rural young men and women and migrant workers. They flock to the app to gain attention and approval, to take a shot at becoming famous on the internet and to find people like themselves that they can relate to.

Women account for the majority of users at 57.8%. 66.6% of users are under 24 years old while 19.6% are 25-30 years old. Some reports conclude that 70 percent of Kuaishou's users earn less than $460 per month and that 88 percent have not attended university.

KOL Promotion

Brands that succeed on this platform are generally in the fast moving consumer goods (FMCG) category such as snacks and beverages or grassroots small businesses. Popularity is decided by viewers so it churns out memes and fads. Content needs to catch viewer attention quickly in clever or striking ways. It's a platform that showcases grassroots creativity and concerns.

Behind the Scenes at Small Businesses and Farms

One model that is popular on the app is "A Day in the Life" style videos that show what goes on during a farmer's average day or how someone makes a famous dish or sauce. This could be used by small business owners in other countries willing to show what things are like behind the scenes and how they live and work day to day.

Eat, Drink and be Merry

Food and drink are very popular on Kuaishou. Harbin Beer took advantage of this and cooperated with 5 Kuaishou KOLs to promote its new easy-open glass bottles. Each KOL used their own unique way to show it to their audience. The uniting factor was that most of their fans were in northeast China. The total exposure added up to 33.79 million post views and 21.11 million video views. 9.326 million fans participated and the number of likes reached 214,000.

Sponsored Dancing, Singing and Rapping

New dancing and singing memes pop up on the app regularly. Regional styles of rapping, like one called "mic-shouting" that's popular in the northeast, have also become big on the app. Brands need to be on the ball to catch them, if they're appropriate and fit the brand's image and purpose. Some brands have sponsored up and coming singers, rappers or dancers who have become popular on the site.

3.6 Yizhibo

Overview

Officially launched in May 2016, Yizhibo is a mobile live-streaming app. As viewers watch, they can interact by commenting, asking questions or by sending digital stickers that they purchase, such as balloons, expensive cars or diamond rings, as gifts. These bloggers and celebrities can then exchange the gifts for money. On average, the app takes a commission of 50-60%.

Since 2015, live streaming has become a growing trend on Chinese social media, and there are over two hundred live streaming platforms on the market. Apart from Yizhibo, two of the better known ones are Inke (映客) and Huajiao (花椒直播). Compared to them, Yizhibo has the competitive edge because it's owned by Weibo and used widely on the app.

As the official live streaming service provider for Weibo, Yizhibo is used by many celebrities and bloggers who have official Weibo accounts. There are now more than 3,000 celebrities and KOLs registered on Yizhibo.

Broadcasts are categorized according to location, popularity, topic, etc. When users join a live stream, they can leave messages any time to interact with the broadcaster. The message pops up on the screen as soon as it's sent and can be seen by viewers and the broadcaster, who can respond to it. Broadcasters earn money when virtual gifts, like pictures of cars and yachts, are purchased and sent by viewers.

When users live stream on Yizhibo, they can share it to their personal Weibo pages as a single post. Once it's shared on Weibo, everyone can watch it, even without Yizhibo installed.

Brands can easily launch a live stream and share it with their Weibo followers. Several brands such as Audi, Samsung and L'Oréal have already used live streaming as part of their marketing activities and there's no doubt that more and more international and domestic brands will incorporate Yizhibo into their marketing mix.

User Demographics

As of September, 2017, it had around 60 million monthly active users. They launched the app on their mobile devices 3.7 times per day on average and spend nearly half an hour every day on it.

Statistics provided by Beijing-based internet consultancy Analysys show that, as of January 2018, 53.9% of users were female and 46.1% were male. Young adults between 24 and 35 years old made up the largest group, accounting for nearly half of the users on the platform.

As for regional distribution, most users are from Guangdong, Shandong and Hebei, and nearly 40% are from first-tier cities, with its biggest popularity in Beijing, Shanghai, Guangzhou, Chongqing, Chengdu, Hangzhou and Xi'an.

Users spend only a few seconds deciding whether they're interested in a stream and switch to another channel almost immediately if not. Broadcasters need to create strong content that can grab viewer attention instantly, build a community that seeks out their streams or publicize streams in advance to ensure a dedicated audience.

Since users have more free time in the evenings, it's a much better time for live streaming. Viewer numbers increase, they watch individual streams for longer and they're more active in terms of engagement. For many, it's a way to relax and connect with others after work.

KOL Promotion

The following are the most common types of key opinion leader live streams.

Product Placement / Embedded Advertising / Sponsored Streams

Brands can give KOLs products to use or wear during live streams. This model would fit clothing brands, audio-visual equipment manufacturers or food and beverage brands best. Brands can also sponsor a popular broadcast and have their logo featured or have the broadcaster announce that the brand is the sponsor and talk briefly about their products.

Destination Live Streams

Brands in the travel, tourism and hospitality fields would do well to launch live streams featuring KOLs and the #Traveling with Weibo# tag. Often, thought leaders act as tour guides and take viewers to visit landmarks or showcase unique restaurants or hotels. They can talk about their experiences, recommend day trips and work with brands to offer discounts or coupons. They can also cover any cosmetics, fashion, accessories, food and lifestyle products that can be used while travelling.

Event Live Streams

From big international events like the Olympics and the World Cup to the grand opening of a physical store, Yizhibo and Weibo can promote them and let people experience the live atmosphere. With opinion leader participation, audience attention is maximized.

Red carpets and fashion shows are audience favourites. People also like to follow celebrities backstage and have a closer look behind the scenes. Audiences are keen to know the stories and daily routines behind the brands they enjoy. This is a particularly effective way to engage with customers and enhance brand credibility

Infomercial / HSN (The Home Shopping Network) Style Broadcasts

With the popularization of live streaming, more e-commerce entrepreneurs have started to use them. They can be very effective for demonstrating products, especially when there's a new release. Customers can buy the items on Taobao or the brand's own website by clicking links in the livestream's description. These live streams enable more direct communication and allow customers to be the first to get their hands on the latest products or to get a big discount.

3.7   Taobao Live

Overview

Taobao Live is a live streaming platform launched in March, 2016 by Taobao, the largest e-commerce platform in China operated by the Alibaba Group. It offers an in-depth opportunity for online retailers to interact with potential consumers and promote their products in a way that combines entertainment and e-commerce. Any Taobao store with a one diamond reputation and more than 10,000 followers can apply to set up their own live stream channel.

Taobao Live appears as a channel on the homepage of Taobao's app and functions in some ways as an e-commerce platform on its own. It's perfect for the "See Now, Buy Now" model where users can purchase instantly while watching a live stream. They don't even need to leave, the platform to complete the purchasing process. For Americans, it approximates the shopping experience of the Home Shopping Network (HSN), QVC or late night infomercials.

The key to the success of Taobao Live is that it grasps the successful formula of "Celebrities/KOL + live streaming + e-commerce". Taobao's huge user base is a major advantage as Taobao Live can reach millions of active users without having to drive traffic from external platforms.

User Demographics

As Taobao doesn't have a separate app for Taobao Live, we'll refer to Taobao users. Statistics from Analysys show that, as of January 2018, there were 425 million active users on Taobao, with over 142 million daily active users.

70.9% of Taobao users are female and 29.1% are male. Women are more interested in clothing, cosmetics, and maternity products while men are more likely to look for electronic products and sportswear. Young adults aged from 24 to 30 years old account for 43.8% of all users. A typical user launches Taobao on their mobile device 4.6 times per day and spends around 25 minutes each day on the app.

Around 80% of live stream viewers on Taobao Live are female and the best time slot for live streaming is between 8 and 10 pm.

KOL Promotion

Celebrity or KOL engagement is very common in Taobao Live. Many brands have successfully enhanced their exposure, attracted more followers and boosted sales thanks to the influence of KOLs.

There are several ways to work with KOLs on Taobao Live.

Product Showcasing

This is the most common and most straightforward way to promote a product on Taobao and very familiar to readers who know the Home Shopping Network and QVC presentation style. KOLs use the products in front of the camera, describe it and answer questions raised by interested buyers to give viewers a better understanding of the product.

Lectures and Q&A

These are usually done by bloggers with professional expertise. They explain the functions of a product or how to maximize its effects. Sometimes they give tips and suggestions and then recommend useful products. After the lecture, viewers can ask questions and interact with the KOL.

Scenario-based Product Promotion

This is an embedded advertising or product placement approach where the product isn't promoted directly. Instead a scenario is designed with the brand in mind. For example, a food blogger can launch a live stream showing how to bake cookies and talk about the features of the oven while showing the viewers how it works.

Product Origins Showcases

In order to increase brand prestige and help consumers develop a deeper understanding of and trust in their products, some brands invite KOLs to visit their factories and show how their products are manufactured from raw material selection to final product. Similarly, some overseas shoppers also film themselves looking for and purchasing items abroad.

3.8   Mafengwo

Overview

Established in 2006, Mafengwo is China's best-known social travel platform. It's similar to TripAdvisor. It debuted as a community for travellers to share their travel itineraries, experiences, tips and useful information about travel destinations, hotels, restaurants, transport, etc.

Now users can browse and download one of the 1million travel guides for destinations all over the world. They can write comments, contribute tips, rate places of interest, hotels and restaurants and ask questions for other travellers to answer. They can also book hotels, train tickets, flight tickets and travel packages.

It's a trusted resource and "Travel Bible", especially for younger, independent travellers who rely on the platform when choosing travel destinations and planning their itineraries.

According to statistics provided by the platform, by the end of 2017, there were over 130 million registered users on Mafengwo with 8.5 million monthly active users. Over 80% of users accessed the platform via mobile devices. In 2017, the gross merchandise volume of Mafengwo reached nearly 10 billion RMB.

User Demographics

Statistics also show that, as of January, 2018, 61.6% of Mafengwo users were female and 38.4% were male. Young adults between 24 and 30 years old made up nearly one third of the users on the platform.

Nearly 20% of Mafengwo users are from Guangdong and over 40% come from first-tier cities, including Guangzhou, Beijing, Chengdu, Shanghai, Shenzhen and Chongqing.

The majority of Mafengwo users are middle-class or high-end consumers with relatively high consumption capabilities who are willing to spend more on travel, lifestyle and luxury products.

KOLs on Mafengwo

As Mafengwo is a social media platform for travellers, KOLs on the platform are mostly veteran travellers or travel bloggers. There are several types of verified accounts on Mafengwo. With this verification system, top

KOLs, or "Da Ren", can be easily identified.

Adviser Accounts (马蜂窝攻略号)

Adviser Accounts are for content producers who can publish travel guides on their own homepage as a verified travel adviser. Organizations or individuals who produce consistent high-quality content can apply for this type of account.

Verified Destination Guide (目的地指路人)

Users who have a lot of travel experiences and are familiar with certain places can apply to be a "Guide (指路人)" for that place and share tips and insider information about it. "Verified Destination Guide" is a higher rank. These users have a blue "V" icon displayed beside their username.

Corporate Accounts (企业号)

Eligible tourism boards, airlines, brands and other corporations can get their accounts verified and set up official pages. Verified corporate accounts also have a blue "V" icon displayed besides user name.

KOL Promotion

Travel Diaries

Most travel bloggers write long travel diaries to talk about their trip, offer practical tips and make recommendations about where to go, eat and have fun. Some bloggers produce videos too. Brands can invite travel bloggers to include a mention of their brand in their travel diaries. Bloggers can also write about highlights or upcoming discounts to help brands attract potential customers.

Destination Reviews

The most popular posting format on the site are destination reviews. Brands should monitor the travel plans of popular KOLs and can invite them to their hotel, theme park or restaurant. A good review can mean repeat business and even more visitors in the future.

Q&A

Mafengwo also has a Q&A function. Just like on Zhihu, the Chinese version of Quora, users on Mafengwo can ask travel-related questions and wait for other users to answer. This Q&A function can also be used for KOL promotions. Brands can invite KOLs to include mentions of the brand or their travel products in their answers to designated questions.

3.9   Platform-specific Case Studies

Xiaohongshu

Fabric softener brand Downy worked with up and coming actress Lin Yun. She talked about how to use Downy and its advantages on her personal homepage which triggered a lot of discussion. In the second round of the promotion, Downy cooperated with more than 50 KOLs who quickly followed the trend, resulting in widespread attention. During the promotion period, Downy's sales volume on Tmall significantly increased.

Douyin

Some KOLs, called "技术流" (Jishu Liu), use unusual skills to get attention. These kinds of videos easily garner attention and start trends. Chinese electronic brand Honor, a Huawei sub-brand, cooperated with popular Douyin KOL 薛老湿 to create a video featuring an optical illusion of his phone floating magically in the air which was reposted and imitated thousands of times.

Videos featuring "finger dancing", where people do fast complex hand and finger movements in time with music, were very popular on Douyin for a time. KOL and popular dancer Mr.three, who has 1.29 million followers, used his finger dancing skills when he cooperated with fashion brand GreenPanda on a finger dancing video featuring the brand that got very high view numbers.

Douyin challenges are hashtagged requests or missions issued on the site. Brands can use them for user-generated content campaigns and to help increase brand awareness. Michael Kors, the American fashion label, was Douyin's first partnership with a luxury brand. In addition to hiring 3 fashion influencers, with a collective follower base of 4 million, to appear at an event with the brand's ambassadors, including Yang Mi and Mark Chao, they promoted a "City Catwalk" hashtag (Douyin hashtags are placed before and after the words in Chinese) challenge by sharing videos of them on the catwalk wearing Michael Kors. The trio's clips were streamed for over 5 million times, with 41,000 users posting their own 15-second catwalk videos using the hashtag.

Kuaishou

Kuaishou features lots of bloggers who showcase niche skills or specialize in niche broadcasting forms such as mukbang videos. The trend for these kinds of videos began in Korea and the name translates roughly as "foodcast". These are usually live streamed and feature people eating large amounts of food as they interact with viewers and sometimes talk about how the food was prepared, the ingredients and so on. 深圳小老虎 is a mukbang blogger based in Shenzhen with more than 180,000 followers. He's a senior gourmet who discovers the best restaurants in Shenzhen and Hong Kong. He often goes to well-established restaurants and makes detailed comments about the location, environment, food preparation and the signature dishes as he eats. He's cooperated with many restaurants in Shenzhen and HK.

Yizhibo Live Streaming

During the International Fashion Weeks in 2016, Yizhibo collaborated with ELLE, Vogue and Marie Claire. They invited fashion icons like Li Yundi, Ma Su and Zhang Xinyu, to stream various shows and events. The audience could follow these celebrities and watch live catwalk shows, go backstage and have a closer look at the clothes. Since then, Yizhibo has become one of the most important promotion channels in the fashion industry.

For New York Fashion Week in September 2016, Coach invited Tang Yan and Li Yifeng, two famous Chinese celebrities, to do a live stream of their visits to the Coach showroom. The two live streams accumulated over 3 million views and 7 million interactions in total. These impressive results show the power of live streams to attract and involve the audience.

Taobao Live

In early 2018, Taobao Live cooperated with Hunan TV and produced a jewellery show live stream. Well-known brands like Chow Tai Fook, Tianbao Longfeng, Laomiao and Mclon participated. Remarkably, Chow Tai Fook's pieces sold out a few minutes after the show and achieved a record of a turnover of 100,000 RMB (14,000 USD) in one minute.

In September 2016, KFC opened its flagship Tmall store and launched a live stream featuring KOLs like Ma Weiwei, Xiao Xiao and Yan Rujin. The live stream video accumulated a total of over 25,000 views. Tide has also successfully launched live streams on Taobao and Tmall. In addition, Maybelline invited famous Chinese actress Angelababy to do a live stream on Tmall, which resulted in the featured lipsticks being sold out.

Mafengwo

In July 2018, Mafengwo cooperated with travel blogger and rap singer Sun Bayi to produce a series of six video travel guides about Rongjiang, an ancient county in Guizhou in the southeast of China.

In the videos, Sun Bayi rapped about unique characteristics of the local culture and the highlights of folk tourism in Rongjiang. The video series was well received, especially by young travellers and the first video was played over 100,000 times. The posts also got lots of comments and many commenters said they'd like to visit Rongjiang some day.

"Behind each KOL, there's a group that recognizes each other's values and sense of aesthetics. But nowadays, social media is layered, fragmented and barriers are going up so it's more difficult for brands to find the best bloggers in their circle than any time before."

— Becky Li,
Highly Influential Fashion WeChat and Weibo Blogger

How It All Fits Together

So, to sum up, here are some platforms, KOL characteristics and industry matches as a quick reference to help you decide on potential partnership models for your business.

The following are all C2C or B2C platforms. B2B platforms are covered in Chapter 6.

WeChat

Type of platform	semi-public social network and microblog
Audience numbers and characteristics	1.04 billion monthly active users (MAU), 797 million monthly active users of official accounts, which are for brands and companies Male vs. Female: 67.5% vs. 32.5% users primarily are aged 18-35, Tier 1-2 cities
Popularity among KOLS	very important
Main form of content	articles, pictures
Cooperation formats	advertorials, product placement, embedded marketing, product reviews, sponsored campaigns, co-branding, KOL cross-promotion, sales on KOL WeChat stores
Most suitable industries	Most B2C brands
Required budget	$$$$$

Weibo

Type of platform	public microblog
Audience numbers and characteristics	431 million MAU, 190 million daily active users (DAU) Male vs. Female: 56.3% vs. 43.7% users primarily are aged 18-30, tier 2-4 cities
Popularity among KOLS	crucial, very popular
Main form of content	posts, videos, pictures
Cooperation formats	sponsored posts, product reviews, giveaways, privilege codes, campaigns, social selling, live streaming
Most suitable industries	Most B2C brands
Required budget	$$$

Xiaohongshu

Type of platform	product recommendation and review community
Audience numbers and characteristics	30 million MAU Male vs. Female: 12% vs. 88% users are aged 18-35, tier 1-2 tiers
Popularity among KOLS	important, very popular
Main form of content	posts, pictures
Cooperation formats	sponsored posts, product reviews, recommendations
Most suitable industries	cosmetics, skin care, baby care, luxury items, food, travel, fitness
Required budget	$$

Douyin (Tik Tok)

Type of platform	music-based short video app
Audience numbers and characteristics	300 million MAU, 150 million DAU (within China) 500 million MAU (including international users on Tik Tok) Male vs. Female: 34% vs. 66% 75.5% of users are under 24, tier 1-2 cities
Popularity among KOLS	very popular
Main form of content	short videos, challenges, live streaming, merchandise promotions, links to Taobao
Cooperation formats	sponsored posts, product reviews, recommendations
Most suitable industries	new/trendy brands, fashion, alcohol, digital electrical appliances, food and beverage, snacks
Required budget	$$$$

Kuaishou

Type of platform	video and live streaming app with a Reddit style system that allows the community to pick popular content
Audience numbers and characteristics	120 million DAU, 230 million MAU Male vs. Female: 57.8% vs. 42.2% 66.6% of users are under 24, tier 2, 3 and 4 cities
Popularity among KOLS	popular among grassroots users outside of major centres not very popular among mainstream KOLs
Main form of content	short videos, live streaming
Cooperation formats	sponsored posts, product reviews, recommendations
Most suitable industries	digital electrical appliances, cosmetics, food and beverage, packaged snacks
Required budget	$

Yizhibo

Type of platform	video sharing and live streaming app, partnered with Weibo
Audience numbers and characteristics	partnered with Weibo which has 431 million MAU and 190 million daily active users (DAU) 60 million MAU Male vs. Female: 53.9% vs. 46.1% most users are aged 24-35, 40% from tier 1 cities
Popularity among KOLS	very popular
Main form of content	live streaming
Cooperation formats	product placement, embedded advertising, sponsored streams, destination live streams, event live streams, infomercial and Home Shopping Network-style broadcasts
Most suitable industries	Most B2C brands
Required budget	$$$

Taobao Live	
Type of platform	live streaming e-commerce app for Taobao
Audience numbers and characteristics	425 million active users on Taobao, 142 million DAU Male vs. Female: 29% vs. 71%. Most users are aged 18-34
Popularity among KOLS	popular for e-commerce and live streaming KOLs
Main form of content	live streaming
Cooperation formats	product showcases, product origin showcases, lectures, Q&A, scenario-based product promotions
Most suitable industries	clothes, cosmetics
Required budget	$$

Mafengwo	
Type of platform	TripAdvisor-style travel recommendation and review platform
Audience numbers and characteristics	100+ million MAU Male vs. Female: 38% vs. 62% users are aged 24-30 (33%), over 40% are from tier 1 cities
Popularity among KOLS	popular
Main form of content	articles, videos, pictures
Cooperation formats	travel diaries, destination reviews, Q&As
Most suitable industries	Travel and tourism, airlines, hotels, resorts
Required budget	$$$

CHAPTER 4

How to Find and Select the Right Influencer for You

With the expansion of social media platforms and accounts on each one, the number of influencers and their followers continues to grow. With the expanding influence and value of KOLs and shifting popularity and reliability, how can brands find the right influencer for them? This chapter offers some practical tips to help brands in that mission.

4.1   Finding and Auditing KOLs

Before working with an influencer, it's important to find a good match. Finding genuine, reliable and suitable KOLs with authentic influence takes some groundwork. Here are some ways you can find and assess an influencer.

WeChat

WeChat's search bar

If you type keywords in WeChat's search bar and choose to only show results for official accounts, you'll see a list of official accounts based on the search keyword.

Note that there are two different categories of official account on WeChat: individual and company-managed.

Individual Accounts: Followers have a greater sense of familiarity and rapport with the blogger behind the account. They're usually seen as reliable with stricter standards when selecting brands to cooperate with. They need to maintain their reputation and content quality.

Company-Managed Accounts: Most accounts run by KOL management companies are verified and have the management company's information shown on the profile page. Sometimes, there are several verified accounts under the same name, up to a maximum of 50. Brands can consider advertising on more than one of the company's accounts as they may offer discounts for promotions that include more than one of their accounts. These accounts are generally more open to advertising and are more likely to accept hard sell advertising approaches.

KOL Marketing Agencies

You can also find KOLs through marketing agencies and online databases that specialize in connecting brands with suitable KOLs. There is a list of agencies for your reference in the Appendix.

Online Databases

There are also companies that manage KOL databases. Users can select KOLs by industry or interest category and promotion budget. Databases specializing in WeChat accounts and content include Sougou, simplyKOL and gsdata.

With the help of these databases, users can get the latest data on the number of followers, total article views and other important statistics. Some also list the price range for cooperation. This can information can also give you a clearer idea of how competing brands are managing their influencer collaborations.

These databases operate like search engines with keywords and filters to narrow searches. When you click on an account, detailed statistics are shown. Other related accounts are recommended and some online databases have an option to leave your contact details for influencers to contact you directly or to get a quote for the costs of promotional cooperation.

Weibo

Verified KOLs on Weibo have an orange "V" icon beside their ID. It's easy to find famous names on the site but finding an influential KOL who fits your marketing needs takes a little more work. Here are a few ways to do it.

Weibo's Search Bar

When you search Weibo with industry-specific keywords, related KOL accounts are displayed. For more detailed searches, you can use the advanced functions, which give you options to narrow results by location, account type, gender and age.

For example:

- Type "时尚"(fashion) or "潮人" (fashion icon) in the search bar
- Select Location: Shanghai only

- Select Account type: verified individual account only

- Gender: Male

- Age: 30-39

A lot of KOLs provide their contact information in their profile or bio. If not, you can still send them a private message and tell them who you are and what kind of promotion you're looking for. Enquiries will be handled by the bloggers, their agents or management companies.

KOL Marketing Agencies

Alternatively, you may choose to contact a KOL by searching on Weibo. You can ask whether he/she is an individual blogger and whether the account is managed by a company. If the account is company-managed, they'll likely provide you with a list of relevant accounts that they're also managing and may also give you advice on which KOL accounts would be best for your brand promotion.

A competitor's choice of bloggers can give you insights on which KOLs, or which type of KOLs, you need to work with, and their effectiveness.

Wei-Task

It's important to note that all Weibo campaigns, particularly those with large KOLs and those that include links to outside sites, must be registered through the Wei Task platform. Campaigns that aren't registered through the platform run the risk of being taken down.

On Wei Task, you can find and select registered Weibo bloggers to repost commercial content. Before you find the KOLs you need to submit a simple plan indicating the price, content and posting time. If the blogger accepts the terms, he or she will promote the content based on the agreed schedule and get paid by the system once the task is completed.

Since it's managed by Weibo, all content is moderated to meet Weibo's regulations. However, due to automation, the platform doesn't advise on which blogger is best for your specific promotion and sometimes recommends ineffective or irrelevant bloggers so do your research beforehand.

Taoboa List Index

Brands can also consult the Weibo account 淘榜单, where a variety of lists featuring the top broadcasters on Taobao Live are published regularly for brands' reference.

These lists provide brands with a ranking of broadcasters' influence by their Taobao List Index (淘榜单指数), which is usually calculated by their live stream views, content quality the ability to drive traffic or attract new followers, as well as viewer interactions. Some lists show the popularity of broadcasters and identify the most promising new ones, while others feature broadcasters in diverse industries, such as fashion, gourmet and so on. With the help of these lists, brands can find the most suitable broadcaster on Taobao Live.

*See the Appendix for a list of KOLs by industry.

Auditing KOLs

Aside from famous bloggers, there are low-key KOLs who have a strong connection with their fans. There are also KOLs who have no influence but create a false sense of popularity with fake followers and interactions. So what are some practical ways to determine a KOL's level of influence and how well their numbers and image match their real world presence? Here are some recommended steps to follow and some key questions to ask.

Check the KOL's profile. Do they post regularly? Do they only post ads or commercial content? Are their interactions and comment related to their content? A good KOL posts with a consistent tone and approach on a regular basis. If they don't post regularly or only post commercial content, they're not recommended. Check their previous articles to see the average article views, likes and comments. If their interactions, reposts and comments are inconsistent, non-existent or not related to the blogger's content, they're not recommended.

Are the average interaction numbers for regular posts similar to those with commercial content? If so, the interactions are likely real. If not, the KOL may be using fake followers to boost their interaction numbers.

When you reach out to KOLs, ask them to give you a few examples of previous cooperations with other brands and the corresponding statistics. You can also ask them to provide screenshots of their account performance statistics from their account management page to get a better idea of their audience and reach.

4.2   Selecting and Evaluating KOLs

New vs. Well-established Brands

Brands often have the misconception that they should only work with famous KOLs. They focus on a blogger's follower numbers and aim for the widest reach possible. But big bloggers aren't always the best choice because their fan base is relatively broad and large followings don't necessarily mean better engagement.

Brands should choose KOLs based on their audience relationship and their awareness among Chinese consumers. For newcomers to China, they should pick KOLs who can bring them exposure to relevant audiences and potential customers. Well-established brands should strengthen their relationship with consumers who are already aware of them.

If you're just entering the China market and have an adequate budget, you might initially allocate most of your marketing budget to top-tier influencers who can instantly bring credibility and awareness, both among consumers and smaller KOLs. Once your brand is known, it's easier to engage with mid-tier and micro-influencers on a large scale and do product seeding more effectively.

On the other hand, if you have a modest budget, it's better to focus on niche markets. A medium-sized KOL with followers who are more relevant to the brand can drive better marketing results. And working with several small KOLs with around 10,000 followers leads to multiple touch points and a better engagement rate with a more loyal audience.

Well-established brands should consider working with super fans and long-tail influencers with dedicated niche audiences to establish a closer relationship with consumers.

"Many brands are going straight for the big-name celebrities or higher profile KOLs, and paying more as a result, but missing an opportunity to develop relationships with smaller influencers who are truly creating tribes out of their followers who all have very specific tastes and interests."

— Jessica Rapp, Senior Writer, Jing Daily

The KOL industry in China is fast-changing and there are tons of rising and falling stars on social media. Brands should choose KOLs that fit their marketing needs, rather than blindly picking the hottest influencer of the moment. As social media evolves and becomes more segmented, everyone will become a mini-influencer who does word-of-mouth marketing for brands they like. The key to KOL marketing in the future won't be working with the most powerful influencer, but motivating micro-influencers to spread the word in an authentic way.

Evaluating KOL Promotions

Promotions can be evaluated in terms of the following parameters:

- Post views

- Likes

- Comments

- Follower growth

- Shares (data to be provided by the KOL)

- Number of hyperlink clicks (data to be provided by the KOL)

- Sales (for sales promotions, especially if trackable purchase links or codes are used)

But keep in mind that most KOLs won't commit to preset KPIs that haven't been discussed or negotiated beforehand. They will usually give you information about their audience and share statistics of previous promotions for your reference. If you have strict KPI expectations, please communicate them to the influencer and agree on them through discussion before paying for a promotion.

4.3   KOLs with Fake Followers

Although buying fake followers, comments and reposts is prohibited, it's still common. Fake accounts, known as Shuijun (水军 "water army"), are managed by bots, click farms or people who are paid nominal amounts to make posts, likes or comments. They're created for or purchased by accounts that want large follower bases and high engagement rates in order to look more popular. Some bloggers and marketing agencies also purchase them to reach KPI targets set by clients.

On Taobao, the popular online shopping site, when you search using keywords such as "weibo" (微博) and "fans" (粉丝), you'll find thousands of providers selling fake followers, reposts, comments or likes. Generally, the more expensive they are, the more difficult it is to identify them as fake. Some providers of fake followers even allow you to specify the location, sex and other parameters of fake followers.

Spotting KOLs with Fake Followers

Although it's sometimes difficult to spot fake fans and comments, there are ways to check. Click on the account holder's follower list if possible. Also click on likes and comments. Check the commenter and liker accounts. Take a look at the following:

Account Name - Fake followers usually have uncommon or nonsensical names, such as a combination of random numbers or English letters.

Profile Picture - Many fake accounts use low-resolution images as their profile picture, have profile images that seem too perfect or leave their profile picture blank.

Posts - If the first few posts of the account are random, meaningless or obviously copied, it's likely fake. Usually fake comments have a similar sentence structure and the content has no relation to the original post.

If the number of reposts, comments and likes of certain posts jumps suddenly, they may be fake. The opposite is also true. Platforms conduct searches for fake followers and delete them regularly so if you find a blogger you've been working with has a sudden drop in follower numbers, it's a warning sign.

Brands and companies cooperate with well-known bloggers to connect with an interactive community, raise brand awareness, build their brand image, introduce products, increase sales and more. If most followers on a blogger's account are fake, it's meaningless to work with them and the work put into content and campaigns will never bear fruit.

4.4   Fees and Payments

Each KOL has his or her own payment scheme, depending on the number of followers and level of influence but in general, asking an influencer to create text, visual or video content or place the brand's post in a prominent position commands higher prices.

The majority of KOLs and their agencies take payments through Alipay. Bank transfers are also accepted but not preferred, as it usually takes a longer time to clear so it's best to open an Alipay account before doing any promotions. Most bloggers in China require 100% prepayment and will only begin promoting after payment has been received.

For small-scale cooperations, with a contracted amount below 15,000 RMB (2,160 USD), bloggers rarely sign official agreements. The usual procedure is to negotiate the terms and pay the full amount prior to the work commencing. Please note that most individual bloggers do not issue legal receipts, called "fapiao" in Chinese, unless you request one. A legal receipt costs approximately 10% on top of the contract amount.

WeChat

WeChat KOLs are generally more expensive to work with than Weibo KOLs.

Size	Followers	Price
Micro-KOLs	less than 10,000 views/article	3,000 to 15,000 RMB (432 to 2,160 USD) per article
Mid-tier KOLs	around 50,000 views/article	15,000 to 80,000 RMB (2,160 to 11,500 USD) per article
Popular KOLs	over 100,000 views/article	80,000 to 500,000 RMB (11,500 to 72,000 USD) per article

Weibo

Weibo KOLs in general are cheaper than WeChat KOLs.

Size	Followers	Price
Micro-KOLs	less than 100,000 followers	1,000 to 5,000 RMB (144 to 720 USD) per post
Mid-tier KOLs	around 500,000 followers	5,000 to 50,000 RMB (720 to 7,200 USD) per post
Popular KOLs	over 1,000,000 followers	50,000 to 300,000 RMB (7,200 to 43,000 USD) per post and up

First tier celebrities, like Angelababy may charge 800,000-3 million RMB (115,000-432,000 USD) per post. Second and third tier celebrities, like Joker Xue (薛之谦), may charge 100,000-500,000 RMB (14,000-72,000 USD) per post.

Popular bloggers and communities, like comedic blogger Aikelili (艾克里里) with 9 million followers, usually charge 50,000-100,000 RMB (7,200-13,000 USD) per post. While smaller KOL accounts, like Lu Xing Xiao Ma Jia (旅行小马甲) with 2 million followers, usually charge 1,000-10,000 RMB (144-1,400 USD) per post.

Other platforms

Xiaohongshu

Size	Followers	Price
Micro-KOLs	fewer than 300,000 followers	3,500 to 7,000 RMB (500 -1,000 USD) per post
Mid-tier KOLs	300,000 to 1,000,000 followers	7,000 to 34,000 RMB (1,000 - 5,000 USD) per post
Popular KOLs	more than 1,000,000 followers	34,000 to 206,000 RMB (5,000 - 30,000 USD) per post

Douyin

Size	Followers	Price
Mid-tier KOLs	500,000 to 1,500,000 followers	10,000 to 34,000 RMB (1,400 - 5,000 USD) per post
Popular KOLs	1,500,000 to 3,000,000 followers	34,000 to 82,000 RMB (5,000 - 12,000 USD) per post

Yizhibo

Size	Followers	Price
Micro-KOLs	50,000 to 200,000	5,000 to 10,000 RMB (750 to 1,400 USD) per live stream
Mid-tier KOLs	around 550,000	15,000 RMB (2,160 USD) per live stream
Popular KOLs	around 1,000,000	35,000 RMB (5,000 USD) per live stream

CHAPTER 5

The Ins and Outs of Effective KOL Campaigns

Before we talk about campaigns and techniques, it's important to know the current situation on the ground in China today and learn more about what KOL campaigns, whether their goal is to boost sales, build awareness or create a database for customer relationship management, can and cannot accomplish.

5.1   The State of the Chinese KOL Industry

Over the past few years, influencer marketing has taken the world by storm, and China is no exception. Local consultancy Analysys International projected that the China influencer economy will be worth over $15.5 billion US this year.

Though influencer brands have been around for many years, Singles' Day really brought them to the public's attention. Singles' Day, November 11th, is a homegrown special occasion for single people that features online shopping discounts. This date was chosen because 11/11 features four ones standing side by side. In 2017, for the first time, influencer brands broke into the top ten best-selling female fashion stores. By the end of the day, a total of six influencer-run stores made it into the Top 30 and four of them made over 100 million RMB (14.4 million USD) in sales.

Ads on TV, print and websites are losing their impact and digital and social channels in China sometimes lack audience targeting tools available in the West. This is why, when done right, influencer marketing is one of the best ways to cut through the noise and reach a specific audience.

For marketers operating in China, collaborating with influencers is an expected and necessary part of their overall marketing strategy. It's not a question of whether or not to collaborate with influencers, but how and when.

Here are some key things brands should know before getting started:

1 Influencer marketing requires a significant budget

In this environment, brands need to allocate more of their marketing budget to KOL marketing. One of the biggest issues brands encounter when entering China is that they grossly underestimate the budget needed for an effective influencer marketing strategy. Without sufficient funding and incorrect budget allocation, they flounder and fail to gain traction. This is especially true in China where even micro-influencers expect to be paid.

Product seeding, or giving away products for free hoping that an influencer will post about it, is a common tactic but it shouldn't be a brand's entire strategy. Even traditionally conservative luxury brands such as Chanel have begun compensating influencers, something they were previously adamantly against. Because product links in posts are restricted on most Chinese social media channels, affiliate marketing and profit share models aren't common and influencers will typically turn them down in favor of campaigns that will pay them outright.

Currently, brands in the US are spending far less than Chinese brands.

Although many US companies have implemented KOL marketing into their strategies, 41% are still spending less than 5% of their marketing budgets on influencer marketing. In China, large companies spend 15-40% of their marketing budgets on KOLs, while small companies allocate about 50-80%. Many foreign brands need to adjust their budget and marketing ideas to fit the situation on the ground in China.

2 The return on investment is lower than you might expect

Not only are costs higher, but the return on investment (ROI) is lower. It's common for foreign brands to have flawed ROI expectations. They apply western standards and key performance indicators (KPIs) to the China market and think that they can get the same results with the same budget they use in their home country. However, China is a much more competitive and expensive market and brands need to increase their marketing investment in order to grab market share.

"Brands still have unrealistic expectations in terms of ROI. For example, they hire a KOL for 50,000 RMB (7,200 USD) and establish a high target for the sales they can make. For new brands, they may need to adjust their expectations. The initial stage is the seed-planting stage where it's important to create word of mouth. Also, most brands want to see a sales response after just one campaign or one post. They need wait for at least 6 months and give it time."

— Elaine Wong, Founder, Double V Consulting

3 Influencer marketing is a necessity and must be done strategically

For newcomers, influencer marketing in China is a completely different ballgame. There are unfamiliar social platforms, distinctive cultural norms and, on top of it all, a language barrier. It's hard to see the whole picture and brands looking for a quick fix can end up disappointed after spending money on the wrong "influencers" or strategy.

4 Make sure you're working with true influencers

An internet celebrity, or wanghong, may be popular, but they're not seen as a trusted source and typically don't hold much influence. Many companies don't do enough preliminary research, end up cooperating with a wanghong who delivers subpar results and are then left with the impression that influencer marketing doesn't work.

Even surveys and news reports, sometimes mix KOLs and wanghong, further clouding understanding. For example, a report co-released by Tencent Social Ads and The Customer Research & User Experience Design Center (CDC) in 2018 surveyed 15,000 of China's Gen Z (post-00s). They asked for their reactions to KOLs. Their responses, showed they value celebrity endorsements as well as influencers and brands they see as trustworthy and knowledgeable but that they put little faith in popular, highly commercial but untrusted internet names who primarily push products.

5 Chinese consumers are increasingly sensitive to overly promotional sponsored content

Poorly executed influencer marketing campaigns have jaded Chinese consumers. As famous entrepreneur Gary Vaynerchuk once said, "Marketers ruin everything." This holds true in China where social media platforms have become flooded with sponsored content.

Brands need to be selective and only work with trusted KOLs who are a good fit. This may take more initial research, but it pays off in the long run. Furthermore, brands need to give KOLs the creative freedom to produce content that they know will appeal to their audience. The softer the sell and the more authentic the content is, the better the reaction will be from their audience.

6   KOL marketing needs to be done on a large scale to be effective

One of the most common reasons that brands don't achieve satisfactory results is that they aren't working with enough influencers. Working with a few KOLs on a one-off campaign won't make significant impact, especially if they're micro-influencers.

An "always-on" influencer marketing strategy done at the right scale is the key to long-term success. This strategy requires collaborating with ten or more KOLs every month and up to 50 in total. If your budget doesn't allow this many actual campaigns, you can do something more foundational, such as sending products. Product seeding can earn exposure for your brand while strengthening relationships with influencers.

It's most effective to collaborate with a variety of influencers who have large and small follower bases. If you're going to engage exclusively with micro-influencers, you're going to need hundreds of influencers to have any real impact. Working with a few dozen isn't going to move the needle.

7   Influencer marketing is not a silver bullet

Brands must recognize that KOL marketing is not a magic solution to all their marketing problems. Influencer campaigns must be part of a holistic strategy that amplifies and optimizes KOL content.

When brand awareness from a KOL campaign is combined with positive e-commerce ratings, a brand's own high-quality content, ads, search engine optimization (SEO), search engine marketing (SEM) and events, brands will achieve much better results.

5.2   Campaign Briefs

Many brands start by selecting KOLs, picking campaign ideas and then head straight into execution, omitting a campaign brief. The biggest reason for the failure of a KOL collaboration is miscommunication between the brand and the influencer. If the two parties don't communicate clearly through the campaign brief, the marketing result will never be great. This is true all over the world, but for Western companies working with Chinese influencers, the stakes are higher due to language barriers, cultural differences and a unique social media and e-commerce ecosystem.

Brands should be aware that China is a very different market where standard Western practices may not apply. China's influencer industry has grown at an incredible pace over the past few years. That means many influencers have seen their audience numbers explode overnight yet they're still in the beginning stages of learning how to work with brands.

If your brand is running a campaign through an office in China or a third-party agency, providing a brief is even more crucial. More parties being involved means a higher chance that someone will miss essential information along the way. To ensure your guidelines and materials are accurate for China, you should have your local agency review and refine the brief before sending it to the influencer.

Before you start, define your goals

Before a brief is even started, brands must be clear about what they want to achieve with their campaign. Most campaigns will have one of the following goals:

1. Increasing brand awareness

2. Increasing sales

3. Building a database of customers / potential customers

These goals will determine multiple aspects of a campaign's nature and execution. It will determine the platforms that the brand needs to use, the influencers they will cooperate with, the campaign formats they will use, the kind of content they will create, sponsor or collaborate on and the KPIs they will need to measure.

Once the goal has been clarified and everyone is on the same page, the brand can then move on to a campaign brief.

Components of an effective campaign brief

A clear and detailed campaign brief should include:

1 A Campaign Overview

Brands should provide an overview of the campaign, including information about the brand, product or service. For example, is it a campaign about a particular product or service, or the brand in general? Is it a social media promotion, an online-to-offline campaign or a standalone event? These are key decisions that need to be made at the start of campaign planning.

2 Campaign Objectives and KPIs (Key Performance Indicators)

Brands should clearly outline the goals of the campaign. Is the goal to increase awareness, promote sales or build a database? What are the specific results you want to achieve? The more the influencer knows in terms of the big picture, the better they can deliver the results. Make sure you tell them the KPIs you'll be using to measure the success of the campaign, such as the impressions, engagements or traffic to your digital platforms. We'll discuss this in more detail later.

3 Content

Brands should identify the key messages, deliverables and style of the campaign. The influencer needs to understand the message you want to convey and the type of content they should create. Is it a video, a photo, a live stream, or a long article? What are the preferred platforms to deliver the content? It's also good to list out the requirements such as the social tags, hashtags or links required, as well as discount codes, landing pages or calls-to-action. Don't forget to set some guidelines around the content theme and style so as to ensure the deliverables align with your brand persona.

4 Do's and Don'ts

Brands should include everything that will help the influencer create the best content and uphold the brand message. You can specify items that you do and do not want to have in the content. For instance, you may want to fix the position of the logo, avoid cultural insensitivity or forbid the inclusion of alcohol or drugs.

Brands should view a campaign brief as a useful summary that empowers the influencer to work creatively. It provides influencers with resources to start conversations about you and your brand. In this way, both parties are on the same page and you can expect to see a thoughtful and effective campaign.

Pre-campaign

KPIs and Metrics

One of the first things that needs to be done, that will set the stage for the rest of the campaign, is defining clear goals and KPIs for the campaign as a whole. Decide whether you want to drive sales, increase awareness or drive offline traffic. Then choose the KPIs that will indicate whether or not the campaign is a success.

> *"Brands need to stand out when running KOL campaigns. Traffic is not enough. Creative campaigns with engaging narratives, leveraging user-generated content, creating limited edition products in collaboration with KOLs, increasing viral power with flash sales and group buys, are only some of the methods that brands can use to increase the efficiency of KOL campaigns."*
>
> — Thomas Graziani, Co-founder of WalktheChat

Your KPIs should then be used to determine which platforms, types of content and KOLs you'll use for your campaign. Brands who do not make sure that their KPIs are aligned with the platform and the KOL are almost guaranteed to be disappointed by the results.

For example, people hear that WeChat has over 1 billion users and think that they must run a campaign on WeChat. But if your KPIs are tied to generating brand awareness through mass reach, WeChat, a closed platform, may not be the best choice. Open platforms like Weibo or Douyin would be a better fit.

Marketers are more than likely already very familiar with some of the common KPIs for influencer marketing campaigns, but not all of the KPIs and metrics used in the west are applicable to China, mainly because less data is publicly available and Chinese social platforms have strict regulations regarding in-post links and brand mentions.

Common KPIs and Metrics

Generating brand awareness and engagement should be key goals of brands new to China. Do people recognize the brand's name and logo? Do they interact with the brand's content? It's also very important when launching a new product. They can be measured in many ways such as impressions, likes, comments, mentions and more. Here's some more detail on how these operate and what they indicate on the ground in China.

Impressions: While impressions are important, they also have to be taken with a grain of salt as it's common for influencers in China and the West to buy fake followers and impressions. There also may be additional costs associated with this KPI. Just as Facebook has restricted the reach for posts on its site, so too has Weibo. In 2018, Weibo's organic reach declined significantly and paid promotion is a way for influencers to ensure their post gets to their audience. Paying to promote a post can be very useful and can dramatically increase impressions with real Weibo users. It also allows the influencer to choose a target audience.

Likes: Likes are the simplest way to measure content appreciation. They also help you quantify the buzz around your influencer content. All of China's major social media platforms include the ability to like a post.

Shares: Shares are another indicator of content quality. If people recommend your content to their social media circles, they're more likely to recommend your products too. Shares are extremely important for posts on Weibo and WeChat as they can increased your post's reach exponentially. Shares can be useful for getting more views during a live stream, but many live streaming platforms don't display share metrics. Douyin and Xiaohongshu do not allow users to share posts.

Saves: An important metric for Xiaohongshu is Saves. When a user saves a post, it's similar to someone pinning something onto a Pinterest board or saving a post on Instagram. It signals that this user is highly interested in this content and wants to look into it at a later date.

> *"It's hard to achieve the same effects as the past in a highly homogenized environment flooded with advertising. 2018 also saw some other changes such as stricter controls and labelling for promotional content to enhance transparency for the audience.*
>
> *Recently, experts who specialize in analyzing influencer data have observed that interactions for many top-tier influencers suddenly soar at midnight, which isn't normal. Are big brands being cheated? I think it's because of limited specified KPIs, such as only requiring exposure. Measuring the promotion effects of KOLs in multiple dimensions helps to avoid this kind of situation."*
>
> — Yi Li – Marketing Director, BorderXLab and shopping app Beyond

Comments: Comments are truly one of the best forms of engagement, but brands need to look at them carefully. Comments can also be purchased and real ones can indicate how much attention the KOL's followers are paying to the promoted brand or products. For example, if a mommy blogger shares a post about her favorite stroller and it receives hundreds of comments about how cute the baby is, that's not going to do your brand much good. Brands know this, but because of the language barrier, many of them don't take the effort to look at the comments the same way they would with social media channels in their native language.

Brand Mentions: Measuring brand mentions allows you to track where your content is being discussed and amplified. For example, brands often find that after working with top-tier KOLs, mid-tier and micro-KOLs start posting about their brand as well.

Increased Search: As we mentioned, when a Chinese consumer is interested in a brand or product, one of the first things they do is search for it online to learn more. To measure growth in awareness, brands should check for correlations between influencer campaigns and increased searches on WeChat and key search engines such as Baidu. These correlations will likely lag by several months, especially for new brands and for limited campaigns.

Conversions: An increase in followers for branded social media accounts is a strong sign of promotional success. While this could be considered increased brand awareness, I'm putting it in the conversion bucket because in China, someone following your social media account, particularly an official WeChat account, is as close as you can get to having them become an email list subscriber.

In China, consumers don't use email the way we do in the West, and it's extremely rare to see brands asking consumers to sign up for an email list. Instead they ask consumers to follow their WeChat account. Many brands have loyalty programs built into their accounts and reward followers with special deals the way you would an email list subscriber.

Note that on many Chinese social channels, for example Weibo, influencers will be unable to tag your brand account without paying platform fees for sponsored posts, otherwise their post might be taken down or have its reach restricted.

Increased traffic to your online store: If your goal is to drive traffic to your e-commerce store, it may be difficult to do so using a link in a KOL's post. This is partly due to platform restrictions and partly due to consumer behavior.

The type of link that can be included depends on which platform your store is on and which platform the KOL will be posting on. For example, on WeChat you may share links to JD.com and mini programs and on Weibo you may share links to Taobao and Tmall.

Click-through rates tend to be fairly low unless there's a strong incentive for consumers to purchase the item through the influencer's link. Because including links can be tricky for little return, it's sometimes better not to include them in a KOL's post. Instead, let consumers find your store themselves or ask the KOL in the comments.

Although it may not be direct, when a KOL campaign is run properly, brands should see a corresponding spike in traffic. It will typically lag by several days for brands that are already established in the market.

Sales: This is the holy grail. Unfortunately, brands hear stories of top-tier Chinese blogger Becky Li selling out 100 MINI Coopers in minutes and Mr. Bags doing the same with TOD's luxury handbags and think that it's easy to sell in China. But this is not always true.

The majority of influencers are good at generating awareness and sharing reviews and specific information about your brand, but can't guarantee increased sales. That being said, if you're going to strive for sales, make sure your brand has already achieved a significant level of brand awareness in China prior to running a sales-focused campaign.

It can be very difficult to drive direct sales using trackable links so a better way to measure conversions from a particular influencer are individualized promo codes.

The initial results of some independent research into e-commerce patterns has made some interesting findings. They've found that sales for startups and new businesses selling in China typically come 1 to 3 months after a spike in awareness generated from a KOL marketing campaign, an increased index ranking, or an increase in brand and product search activity.

Choosing the Right Platforms for Your KPIs

Once you've chosen your KPIs, you can go about choosing the platforms and content types. One of the biggest challenges for Western brands doing KOL marketing in China is that the social media platforms are different, and they end up selecting platforms that aren't a good fit for their KPIs. Here are some tips for each of the top social media platforms in China:

Weibo

- Due to its open nature it's a great platform for mass brand awareness.

- It can be a good platform for sales, but there are restrictions.

- Posts may only include links to Alibaba affiliated e-commerce platforms.

- Sponsored posts that tag the brand's account and include a link, must be approved through Weibo's influencer agency platform WeiTask otherwise the post's reach may be throttled or the post will be taken down.

WeChat

- Due to its closed nature it's a poor platform for mass brand awareness. It's better for targeted awareness among specific audiences.

- With the development and adoption of e-commerce mini programs, WeChat is becoming a stronger platform for driving sales.

- Links to Alibaba properties are not allowed.

Douyin

- It's a great platform for mass brand awareness.

- Branded challenges provide a unique opportunity for users to engage with your brand.

- Videos are short, between 15 seconds and 1 minute, so brands need to make sure their product is prominent and easily identifiable.

- It's a poor platform for driving sales except for FMCG.

Live streaming apps

- Brands should stick to Yizhibo, Taobao Live, JD Live and platforms that focus on e-commerce live streaming.

- Platforms focusing on entertainment live streaming and virtual gifting will be less effective for sponsored streams. Many of these platforms have a majority male audience.

- Live streaming is an excellent medium for deep engagement, building loyalty and for driving sales, particularly on Taobao Live and JD Live because users of those platforms are in purchasing mode.

Xiaohongshu

- It's an excellent platform for generating brand awareness.

- It's noted for its high-quality engagement.

- You can't include product links unless your product is sold through Xiaohongshu.

- Posts that engage in hard selling will be taken down.

- Because it's used as a product research and recommendation tool by many users, it's effective at driving sales. However, users often make their purchases on another site.

Search Engines

Once you've started working with influencers, optimize their posts for search engines. Search engines index many social media networks' posts, which means that optimized posts can have a significant impact on a brand's searchability.

This means that brands must determine the keywords they want to target and ensure the KOL uses them in the title and throughout the content. Posts should be 500 words or more and backlinks to an original post's URL will increase its search rankings.

Choosing the Right KOLs

Once you've set your KPIs and determined which platforms to run the campaign on, you can begin selecting KOLs.

Ideally you want to find KOLs who have experience creating the type of content you need to achieve those KPIs. If the KOL has hit those targets in the past they're more likely to duplicate that success.

Furthermore, it's crucial that you clearly explain the goals of your campaign to the KOL. He or she can't help you achieve your goals if your haven't clearly communicated them.

An influencer's work isn't done once they send a post out. Influencers are diligent about responding to fan comments. They know that this is one of the best techniques for creating a genuine rapport between them and their audience. Their responses can also be the difference between whether or not someone purchases the products they recommend.

Brand Involvement and Best Practices

Jump In the Comments Section

What many brands fail to do is get involved in the comments on social media. Any time they see an influencer share their products, whether it's a sponsored post or not, brands should be jumping in and replying to comments with their official brand account. Not doing this is a missed opportunity to build a relationship with a customer.

Great Brand Account Content

If you're going to ask an influencer to drive traffic to your brand accounts, you better give their audience a reason to follow you, either with entertaining content or special incentives. It's the influencer's job to get their followers to your account, but you need to keep them there.

Review Results with the KOL

Lots of brands don't follow up with influencers post-campaign. For brands who claim to not be seeing the results from influencer marketing, it may be because they aren't following through and collecting all the appropriate data, evaluating and learning for future campaigns.

5.3 WeChat and Weibo Campaigns

Chinese social media thrives on interactive and interesting campaigns and different platforms require different approaches. We looked at a selection of prominent B2C platforms in chapter 3 and will cover B2B platforms in chapter 7. For this section, we'll only go into detail for the two most important platforms — WeChat and Weibo. Each suits different goals and they also have slightly different rules and regulations. Let's take a look.

WeChat

Launching campaigns on WeChat is the most effective way to increase user engagement. Though WeChat itself doesn't have a function to organize campaigns, brands can still launch them via articles with incentives like discounts or giveaways.

Here's a list of ideas and examples.

Q&A

Question and answer campaigns are best for:

- increasing brand awareness

- building a brand image through storytelling

- increasing account followers, recommendations and soft promotion

The main objective of the Q&A approach is to encourage users to participate after a push article is published. The article discusses a general topic and asks the audience to express their opinions on it or to answer specific questions. It also gives details of the campaign, including the rules, prize information, the deadline, the winner announcement date and the prize distribution schedule. Incentives should be attractive, inviting and connected with the brand.

Option A

A typical call to action is "Follow and comment to participate in a lucky draw".

The account administrator turns on the "followers only" comment function. Only the account administrator can select featured comments and only these comments will be displayed in the comment section below the article.

Methods for choosing winners include:

- picking the comment(s) which impress you the most

- picking the comment(s) randomly

- picking the comment(s) with the most likes (Recommended)

Picking the one with the most likes means people are more likely to share the campaign article and ask their friends to "like" their comments, generating buzz and traffic. It's also strongly recommended to take and publish a screenshot of the comment with the most likes when the campaign ends as proof.

An official congratulating message can be sent publicly under the winning comments. Then ask the winners to send you a direct message to give their personal information and arrange to send them their prize. There can also be an official announcement of the campaign results in the next push article.

Option B

A typical call to action is "Reply to the question in a message to us to participate".

Participants send private messages with their answers. The account administrator checks the messages, chooses the winner and makes an announcement through the official account, either embedded in the next article or sent through a mass direct message.

Offering Special Resources

These campaigns are best for:

- increasing account followers, recommendations and soft promotion

- building a brand loyalty

- building brand status, reputation and thought leadership

Users are constantly looking for useful information and resources such as interview techniques, movie databases, etc. In exchange for certain resources or benefits, users need to follow the official account and share a designated article to their Moments page.

A typical call to action is "Follow and share this article on your Moments page to receive our interview guide".

Resources can be tool kits, learning materials, white papers, reports and more but should be related to the article. The article should also mention the valuable resources your brand offers to followers and should include a detailed description of the resources they will get. A screenshot of the article on their Moments page can be sent by private message to get the resources.

Tests and Quizzes

These campaigns are best for:

- increasing follower participation

- building buzz

- building brand knowledge

Tests and quizzes are popular interactive formats that can be included in articles. We recommend integrating product or brand information into the quiz. There's no function that allows people to click on selected answers within the article so readers must list their answers in the comments or in a direct message to the brand's account. The correct answers can be revealed the following week.

These kinds of quizzes are easy to construct and manage. It's best to make the quiz short and clear so readers aren't discouraged from participating.

Mini Programs and H5 Pages

For a few years, H5 pages, short for HTML5 pages, were the most popular WeChat campaign tool. They were highly visual, single-purpose, interactive pages. They could be integrated into articles to maximize visual impact and attract users. Successful H5 campaigns spread virally and achieved 100,000+ views. However, they're less popular now.

The big boom is now in WeChat mini programs. In contrast to H5 pages, they're multi-purpose and can be used on an ongoing basis for customer relationship management (CRM), e-commerce, marketing and facilitating O2O engagement for offline events. They can increase brand awareness, introduce products and publicize reports or analyses. There's a lot of flexibility in terms of presentation and format and innovative ideas can be executed for quizzes, games, invitation cards, narratives and more.

Mini programs have become so useful that their influence is spreading and other platforms. Platforms like Alipay, Toutiao and Weibo are now making their own mini programs and developing their own mini program ecosystems. Brands would be wise to develop mini programs for these platforms to take care of CRM, build an online store or take care of other customer or brand needs that arise.

Tips for WeChat Campaigns

- Before launching a campaign, first determine its goal and give each campaign a clear focus and objective. It can be to increase brand awareness, boost sales or collect user information and build a database.

- Offering incentives is a key way to achieve higher engagement. The more complicated the campaign rules are, the better the gifts should be. Offer gifts that are related to your brand, industry or the theme of the campaign.

- Choose a suitable duration for the campaign. A WeChat campaign usually lasts for one week in order to achieve optimal exposure and generate participation.

- Launching campaigns for festivals, special events or based on trending issues increases exposure and attracts a bigger audience. Weekends and holidays are the best times to launch campaigns. To make sure you don't miss any important days for promotion, create a marketing calendar highlighting major holidays like Chinese New Year, the Dragon Boat Festival, Mid-Autumn Festival, etc.

- For H5 campaigns, always test them prior to launch and monitor them during the campaign for technical problems or bugs that might allow cheating, especially for campaigns that offer prizes and incentives.

- Regulations for campaigns on WeChat are strict. Brands can't launch any campaigns that ask people to follow certain WeChat accounts in return for incentives.

Weibo

One of the major reasons they follow official accounts on Weibo is to participate in campaigns and win prizes. All Weibo campaigns can be launched free of charge.

There are two major types.

- **System Campaigns**: These are launched using Weibo's system with formats and rules developed by the Weibo team. This function is only accessible to verified accounts.

- **Creative Campaigns**: The rules for these can be defined by the user and are launched from the campaign page. This type of campaign is accessible to both ordinary and verified accounts.

System Campaigns

With a verified account, you can launch a system campaign from your account management centre under the Marketing & Promotion menu.

There are 5 major formats of system campaigns for you to choose from.

1 Repost Campaign

This campaign is the simplest and most straightforward for brands and the most popular for users as it's the easiest way to try to win prizes. Repost campaigns are best for promoting brands, products or services.

Fill in the information for the campaign in your account management centre. This includes the campaign title, its topic in the form of a hashtag (#topic#), the campaign's duration and a promotion poster. Add the campaign's repost message which will be published as a tweet for participants to repost.

You can choose up to 5 prizes and details for each prize, including a picture of each, should be provided. Add a campaign description providing detailed information about the campaign, such as prizes, duration, rules, etc. It can be in either text or visual format.

2 Content Collection Campaign

Content collection campaigns encourage creativity, help brands collect original material and let them gather direct feedback from fans. You can set a unique theme and users can contribute their pictures, videos, feedback, slogans and more. Their original content will be displayed on the campaign page, and the winners will be selected from the participants.

The advantage of these campaigns are that they're strong word-of-mouth generators and motivate potential customers to buy.

3 Lucky Roulette Campaign

These campaigns allow users to spin a roulette wheel for a chance to win prizes. This type of campaign is easy, fun and popular. These campaigns also go well with a diverse range of prizes, from small inexpensive gifts, such as USBs, to highly desirable items like the latest iPhone.

They're set up using the account management centre. Brands choose a campaign title, hashtag and duration. Account managers can also set the frequency of participation for each user from 3 times in total to 3 times per day. Prize details and photos must also be submitted.

The account manager also sets the chances of winning each prize. The top prizes must be set at the lowest (ex. 10%) with each of the lower value prizes set at a progressively higher rate. The total must equal 100%.

You need to provide details on the campaign, prizes, duration, rules and how to receive the prizes.

4 Flash Sales Campaign

Flash sales campaigns allow businesses to promote selected products to their followers at huge discounts for a short period of time. Users just need to press the participation button and they're notified immediately whether they win the discount or not. This type of campaign is best for e-commerce or O2O promotions.

They're set up using the account management centre. Brands choose a campaign title, hashtag and duration.

Flash sales campaigns are similar to lucky roulette campaigns in that users are notified immediately whether they have won or not.

5 Free Trial Campaign

These campaigns allow brands to distribute product samples to their account followers. To participate, followers need to give reasons why they should be chosen. This format works best with desired physical items like cosmetics or electronics.

They're set up using the account management centre. Brands choose a campaign title, hashtag and duration. Trial sample information, along with images, must be given along with a campaign description detailing the campaign, prizes, duration, rules etc.

As for flash sales campaigns, participants need to state a reason why they should receive a free sample. When the campaign ends, participants will be informed of the results.

Creative Campaigns

Creative campaigns allow winners to be handpicked and are accessible to any type of account. They're usually presented and launched with a post and there's a great deal of flexibility in terms of participation method, prizes, number of winners and promotional channels.

Since all the campaign information is provided in text and pictures in a post on a brand's account, KOL involvement or advertising are essential to promote it.

Publish the campaign post, with details of the campaign, prizes, and participation guidelines and encourage followers to repost to win certain prizes. After the campaign has finished, go to the account management center. Click on "Marketing & Promotion" followed by "Lucky Draw Centre". Find the campaign post and click the "Lucky Draw" button to fill in the details and select the winners. The system will conduct it automatically at the set time and the winners will be selected by the system following the criteria chosen. The winners will also be notified by private message and be asked to submit their contact details in order to redeem their prizes.

Weibo system and creative campaigns compared

Eye-catching visual designs, attractive incentives and easy, fun participation formats are the best ingredients for a successful Weibo campaign. Below is a comparison table for System Campaigns and Creative Campaigns to help you decide which one fits your marketing needs.

	System Campaign	Creative Campaign
Account Qualification	Verified accounts only	All accounts
Format	Can be found in the Weibo Campaign Centre (http://event.weibo.com/) and has its own campaign page	A single post found on account profile page.
Materials Needed	Campaign title Campaign topic Campaign period Promotion poster (640x640px in jpg, png, gif format), Campaign description Prizes	Freestyle post format. Details of the campaign can be presented in the format of a Weibo post with pictures or a long Weibo article.
Rules and Regulations	Pre-set by Weibo for different campaign formats. Users just need to specify the requirements before the launch of campaign	Designed by users according to the campaign format. Criteria for selecting the winners can be set by using the Weibo system after the campaign has finished.
Advantages	Campaign format, template and rules are ready-made. It can be offered to a wide audience for participation.	More room for customization and creativity to show uniqueness.
Disadvantages	Some fake accounts can also partake in the campaign.	Advertising and KOL involvement are essential for accounts with a small follower base.

5.4 Rules and Regulations

WeChat

WeChat announced a new set of rules in April 2016. Breaking these rules can result in consequences ranging from blocking the content in question to a permanent ban for the official account. New rules include the following:

1. KOLs must disclose sponsored and marketing-related posts.

2. No soliciting an audience to follow or share. Any posts or messages

that try to coerce people to share or follow the account or entice them to do so by offering incentives such as red packets, coupons, cash, etc. is banned.

3. Games or quizzes cannot be used to entice users. External links to some H5 games and quizzes like personality tests and new year lucky draws, are no longer allowed except those developed by Tencent.

4. No fraudulent or misleading content. Clickbait headlines that don't match the content or mislead users are banned. It's also explicitly forbidden to use fake incentives, like fake red packets, cell phone data credits, etc. to entice users.

5. No spreading of unsubstantiated information. Disseminating false information and rumours, such as claiming that bananas cause cancer, that tap water is poisoned, etc., is strictly banned.

6. No vulgar content. Accounts shouldn't share any explicit sexual content or anything else that is vulgar, violent or abusive.

7. No data collection should be conducted without user consent. Unless users permit the collection of data, an account should not collect their personal information. This includes information such as their name, birth date, ID number, etc. Asking users to submit personal information in order to get access to account content is also not allowed without giving privacy policy details and a consent agreement.

8. No religious donation content. Content that encourages users to donate to religious groups online is forbidden. This includes online sites that allow users to worship Buddha after giving a donation.

Weibo

All content published on Weibo is monitored and regulated both by national authorities and by Sina Weibo. In general, information which is deemed sensitive, harmful to the country's territorial integrity or contrary to China's constitution is not allowed to be displayed on Weibo. Obscenity, indecency, violence, Internet bullying, and privacy intrusions are also not permitted.

Marketing-related posts and campaigns must be managed through Wei Task or will be blocked. Users should not post links or QR codes unless they are for Alibaba and related platforms and QR codes may not be included in photos and videos.

Users are not allowed to publish the following kinds of information:

1. Information that endangers national and community security ("sensitive information" in short) in accordance with existing laws and regulations, which: opposes the basic principles established by the constitution; harms the unity, sovereignty, or territorial integrity of the nation; reveals national secrets; endangers national security, or threatens the honour or interests of the nation, incites ethnic hatred or ethnic discrimination, undermines ethnic unity, or harms ethnic traditions and customs; promotes evil teachings and superstitions, spreads rumours, disrupts social order and destroys social stability; promotes illicit activity, gambling, violence or calls for the committing of crimes; calls for disruption of social order through illegal gatherings, formation of organizations, protests, demonstrations, mass gatherings and assemblies; has other content which is forbidden by laws, administrative regulations and national regulations.

2. Spam and malicious information, mainly as follows: fake trading and falsifying legitimate businesses; making or forwarding harmful comments/messages; fake campaigns, where followers are induced but the prize is not promised; mass advertising posts by an automatic program or by other third-party software; meaningless and repetitive content sent by third-party software.

3. Adult content mainly as follows: erotic pictures, videos, texts or audio of a sexual nature.

Users should be especially cautious about content that might be considered rumour, incitement or information that poses potential harm to China's territorial sovereignty or national unity. According to the regulations, users logging more than 5 posts with "sensitive information" will be suspended from posting for 48 hours and have the relevant content deleted. Furthermore, those users posting "sensitive content" with "malicious intent" will be suspended from posting for more than 48 hours and face possible account termination.

Meanwhile, users should not infringe on copyright by copying others' Weibo posts without attribution and should seek permission when necessary.

CHAPTER 6

KOLs and B2B: How You Can Collaborate Effectively

The previous chapters have been about brands and companies that sell to consumers. This one is for brands that are seeking connections with other businesses.

6.1   B2B Platform Overview

There are several platforms in China that are geared toward business to business (B2B) networking. However, only one, Zhihu, is truly suitable for KOL promotions. This chapter will focus on how to do KOL promotions on that platform. First, here's an overview of other B2B platforms that businesses may want to establish a presence on.

1688

1688.com is an Alibaba B2B e-commerce platform. In Chinese, numbers are often used in expressions and slang because their pronunciation sounds similar to other words or because they symbolize other things.

"1688" / "yi liu ba ba" sounds similar to Alibaba and the numbers 6 and 8 symbolize fortune. Two 8s together are even better. It's also easy to remember and type.

Similar to Alibaba, millions of manufacturers, traders and buyers from all over the world use the site each year. It covers 16 industries including raw materials, industrial products, clothing and apparel, household items and small commodities. It deals with a wide range of services from raw material procurement, production and processing to wholesaling services but it's mostly used for wholesale buying and dropshipping.

As a top B2B platform in the industry, it saw explosive growth in 2018.

Ximalaya FM

Ximalaya is a podcasting service that enables users to share audio and personal radio stations. It was founded in 2012 and launched its app a year later. It soon achieved its target of 10 million subscribers. As of 2018, there are 40 million registered users, 6 million daily active users (DAU) and 10,000 daily podcasts that are often done by professionals and experts in different fields.

Knowledge Planet and Dedao

Knowledge Planet is an educational community app. Formerly known as "Secret Circle", and known in Chinese as "知识星球", it's a tool for content creators to connect with fans, make quality communities and share knowledge.

Launched in 2015, mobile app Dedao is also a learning community networking app. It was launched by Luo Zhenyu. Luo is a former journalist and TV producer with CCTV, who moved from traditional media to become an influential We Media broadcaster with "The Luogic Show", which has over a billion plays for its multimedia content. Paid subscription podcasts are its main product. It has nearly 1.5 million paid subscribers.

6.2   KOLs and B2B

B2C companies face consumers who they can make a connection with built on an emotional foundation. However, B2B businesses face unique challenges in terms of KOL marketing as companies that offer services or products for other businesses. Which social media platforms can B2B businesses use? How can they use KOLs?

The most suitable KOLs for B2B companies are those who are already consulting in the industry or serving potential customers and have a stable relationship with them. These include:

- Senior consultants with decades of industry-specific experience

- Business management consultants

- Heads of industry associations promoting industry-related education

- Analysts in specific industry sectors

- Key suppliers who have been deeply involved in a specific industry

- Knowledgeable workers or former workers in the industry

So B2B KOLs can be any prestigious or knowledgeable industry players. As such, care, attention and transparency must be used when cooperating with them to enable them to maintain their reputation.

Zhihu

Zhihu is an information sharing question and answer platform, similar to Quora. It has a unique community that regulates its content and ensures high standards, giving it its reputation of being reliable, professional and academic.

According to iResearch, 78.2% of its users are 25 years old or older. This is a time when many are looking to expand their career opportunities and knowledge. 80.1 percent of Zhihu users hold a bachelor degree or above. Given this, they likely have higher than average salaries and greater purchasing power than average.

How Can B2B Companies Use Zhihu for KOL Promotions?

There are KOLs on Zhihu, just as on other platforms. They're called Zhihu Big V (知乎大V). Popular Zhihu bloggers produce a great deal of professional generated content. The most followed KOL on Zhihu, Zhang Jiawei, now has 1.73 million followers and another popular poster on the site, Ge Jin, has 660,000 followers as of July 2018.

Those who want to succeed on Zhihu need to have professional qualifications and knowledge to share with the Zhihu community. They also need to be open-minded and be able to discuss topics clearly. In a sense, it's much easier for new KOLs to build a reputation on Zhihu as the value of high-quality content is more important than a KOL's personality.

The other big advantage of Zhihu is that it helps brands rank highly on Chinese search engines. A well-written article on Zhihu that's seen by lots of people can help a brand appear at the top of the results page on search engines like Baidu for years. Reputable, comprehensive pieces on Zhihu often rank higher than articles from mainstream Chinese media.

Who Should Use Zhihu for Marketing?

Zhihu users are searching for practical, reliable information that can help them out in terms of their life, career or health so businesses in the following areas do well using the platform.

- B2B companies

- Information and technology brands

- Professional services like law firms, education providers and medical services

- Lifestyle brands

B2B Companies

B2B companies are very difficult to market on social media and the general public often knows little about them. This is why they usually don't perform very well on top platforms like WeChat or Weibo. However, marketing on Zhihu may be more effective while enabling them to attract potential partners, business clients and fellow professionals.

B2B companies marketing on Zhihu can invite their staff, experts or KOLs in their industry to answer questions for them. Through answering questions and inviting thought leaders to mention the brand when appropriate, B2B companies can showcase their expertise and connect with other companies.

For example, Siemens set up its official account and wrote an article in their Zhihu Column about how cutting edge the manufacturing industry is. The article got more than 1,400 likes and 755 comments.

In another example, Mercer, the global human resources consulting firm, is known for answering questions on the site related to jobs, salaries and careers. One user asked, "Where should we live if we want the same salaries as Beijing, Shenzhen and Shanghai". In their answer, they referenced their *Annual Quality of Living Ranking* report with a playful tone and provided users with a comprehensive answer. By constantly responding to relevant topics with high-quality answers, they demonstrate their expertise and have built a good reputation on the site.

> *"Brands should really try to understand the ways in which a KOL is influential and what role they play in a certain group to figure out what they're going to get out of a collaboration. Not all collaborations have to directly translate to sales. They can go towards establishing a brand awareness and culture that could have bigger benefits in the long term."*
>
> — Jessica Rapp, Senior Writer at Jing Daily

Information and Technology

Zhihu has a lot of super users in the information and technology field. They care about tech trends and want to share the information they have. Another distinguishing factor of Zhihu is its 3H community, meaning they have high incomes, high academic qualifications and hold high professional positions. Tencent used this knowledge to great effect by asking questions like "What do you think were watershed events in the technology industry in 2016?" By asking a compelling question, it gained insight on the topics users care about the most.

Professional Services

Consistently providing high-quality content in a given field is an essential strategy on the site. As a role model in the education industry, HJ (沪江) plays a role as an "English teacher" on Zhihu. In 2017, HJ was named "The Most Influential Agency Account". The account contributed 130+ articles on language learning and culture with titles like *Tips for English Online Meetings* and *Everyday English Sentences*.

Lifestyle Brands

A great example of a lifestyle brand that's active on Zhihu is Nestlé. They held an offline gathering to provide tips for the parents of newborns and facilitate experience sharing. They wove information about their products into the tips showing their benefits for babies and parents. The session was warmly received.

6.3   How Can You Find Zhihu KOLs?

Start by searching for existing KOLs. After years of development since it launched in 2011, Zhihu has lots of users who are very influential in their professional fields. They have plenty of followers and can easily be found via search engines like Baidu or on the platform itself.

Reputable KOLs can also be found if you search for the top answers under specific topics or look for published articles related to your industry that have received the most feedback and recommendations.

Some third party tools, like kanzihhu.com and zhihurank.com, can also be used but they`re not always reliable.

Please also see the Appendix for a link to a list of reputable Zhihu KOLs on Zhihu itself.

Champion New KOLs

As content is much more important than name on Zhihu, it's easier to create new KOLs by contributing quality content. KOLs who are popular on Weibo, WeChat and other platforms can bring their followers to Zhihu if they have expertise to share. Professionals can quickly garner recognition there through their contributions.

"Importantly, micro-influencers have the advantage of being closer to their communities and are, at least for the moment, immune from the negative effects of increased exposure and commercial success."

— Michael Norris,
Consumer Research Manager at Resonance China

6.4 How Can You Work with KOLs on Zhihu?

Zhihu Live

Do a live stream with a KOL on a specific topic. The content should be professional and on a topic that people are keen to learn more about.

Wenda 问答

Most brands start marketing on Zhihu using its basic question and answer function, which is called Wenda in Chinese. Brands can create an organization account. Then they can answer and pose questions to the community to establish a relationship with users and build their reputation.

Brands can also introduce their products with articles and invite KOLs to answer questions related to the brand. For example, Wang Xiaochuan, the CEO of Sogou, who's quite influential on Zhihu, posted 2 articles about Sogou's AI search engine that received hundreds of interactions from technology professionals.

Roundtable 圆桌

Roundtable is an online panel session for guests to share first-hand information about a sector or to discuss a current event with the audience. Zhihu invites a host with at least four years of experience in a field to share their insights, dissect the industry and guide the audience in their career. They are often made available to users for a limited time post-broadcast.

B2B companies can invite KOLs to launch a roundtable to discuss business and brand related questions. Siemens invited thought leaders to hold a roundtable on the topic of Industry 4.0. During the discussion, Siemens introduced the question "Under the influence of German industry 4.0, what changes will the manufacturing industry usher in?". This roundtable content was viewed more than 88,000 times. The discussion increased Siemens's brand awareness and got plenty of engagement from users who joined the discussion. KOLs such as Gou Zidong (郭子动), who has more than 2,000 followers on Zhihu, joined in and one of his answers got 137 agreements.

The costs of KOL marketing on Zhihu are likely to be much more affordable than on Weibo or WeChat. For some thought leaders, payment may not be their first consideration if an association with your brand provides other benefits.

B2B companies can also use their organization account to publish articles. Leading corporations in the B2B field in China, such as Alibaba and JD.com, do this.

Other Marketing Tools on Zhihu

There are other promotional tools available on Zhihu that can be used to complement a KOL engagement strategy.

Organization Accounts

Siemens was the first B2B company to open an organization account. They published articles in their Zhihu Column and answered the questions related to their technology and products. They responded to 25 consumer questions and wrote 27 articles. Now Siemens has more than 24,000 followers, 13,000 approvals and almost 9,000 bookmarks for its articles. One of its articles, about dishwashers, got more than 3,700 likes and nearly 900 comments.

User-generated Content Campaigns

QQ Music launched a UGC campaign on Zhihu for the May 20th 520 Festival. They asked "How would you say *I love you* with a song?" There were 2,083 answers. Some influencers also posted their answers such as famous blogger 有本事你来咩我呀, who has 33,000 followers on Zhihu. Her answer got a lot of attention, partly due to its explicitness, and got 324 agreements.

Native Advertising / Advertorials

Kindle had a strong native advertising campaign on Zhihu. The account published an article entitled *What Can Reading Bring Us*? It began with the words of German writer Hermann Hesse and discussed the intellectual value of reading. It resonated with users who love reading.

Later on, Kindle cooperated with Zhihu KOL Wan Fang Zhong (万方中), who has more than 74,000 followers. He answered a question about why he bought a Kindle.

For B2B companies, Zhihu should be part of a long-term plan. KOL promotion can be a powerful marketing tool to establish long-term trust and thought leadership, but results won't come overnight. However, it's worth noting that Zhihu's native advertising isn't cheap. The minimum budget is 7,000 USD.

CHAPTER 7

What Can You Expect From KOL Collaboration?

7.1   Setting Realistic Expectations

When it comes to influencer marketing, a common question brands ask is, "Is KOL marketing worth the cost?" When done correctly, it is.

"I've seen many brands exploring working with influencers, but without setting clear expectations on how the collaboration should work. Brands should set clear goals before considering working with influencers and question themselves. How does influencer marketing fit into our current marketing strategy? Which channels should we use? What do we expect the ROI to be? This way, a brand creates much more value for an influencer with expectations aligned from the start."

— Fabian Bern,
Founder and Managing Director of Uplab

As mentioned previously, Chinese consumers are becoming increasingly wary of advertising and tend to seek out product recommendations from people they know, like and trust. Working with influencers is the best way to break through the noise and reach your target customer.

To sum up some points that were made earlier in the book, realistic expectations are of primary importance, otherwise brands will be left sorely disappointed. While influencer marketing should be a core component of your China marketing strategy, it's not a silver bullet that will solve all your marketing woes. In addition, it requires a significant budget and the returns on that investment will be different than in other markets.*

*See the Appendix for a link to a campaign cost estimator tool.

Here's some other key information to remember:

1 Put awareness before sales

A common mindset among brands new to China, particularly ones that sell well in their home country, is that working with Chinese influencers can immediately bring them sales.

This is unrealistic. No matter how influential an influencer is, they're not going to be able to sell a brand that has no existing awareness among Chinese consumers. If Chinese consumers search for your item and can't find any information on it, they'll have difficulty trusting it.

Brands hear flashy stories like Mr. Bags selling out hundreds of TOD's bags in minutes and want to replicate this success, but they forget that that wasn't TOD's first influencer campaign. TOD's has been grinding away in the China market for years building their reputation with consumers and developing relationships with KOLs before achieving this level of success with influencer marketing.

Brands new to China should focus on brand building and create a solid foundation before attempting a hard sell.

2 It takes trial and error

It's going to take time and some experimentation to figure out which platforms and KOLs bring you the best results. In the beginning there are likely to be campaigns and posts that are lackluster, even if you work with a top-tier influencer marketing agency. KOLs are people and platforms and consumers are always changing. While you may have done your due diligence, there are many elements of the equation that are out of your control.

Just as you do for any other part of your business you should constantly be iterating. Seek out partnerships with new KOLs, end relationships with ones that don't provide quality results and try out new platforms and content types.

Keep in mind that a KOL may not be able to deliver their best results the first time they work with you. The second time around, they'll better understand your content style and expectations.

3 KOL marketing isn't going to have an effect overnight

As we will discuss later this chapter, brands that take a long-term approach to KOL marketing typically get the best results.

Think about public relations. You can't just work with a PR agency once and expect the job to be done. Your PR person needs to develop and maintain relationships with the media on an ongoing basis and pitch story ideas in the hopes that one day they will hit a home run and get a widely read, great piece of press. The same goes for influencer marketing. A one-off campaign may create a temporary spike in awareness for your brand but will have little to no long-term effect.

KOL marketing might not produce sales immediately, but brands notice a correlation between effective KOL campaigns and increases in searches for the campaigning brand's name on e-commerce sites and Baidu. Sales lag campaigns as consumers need to research the product first and brands need to find the right price point.

Post-campaign Analysis

Here are some of the things brands should do post-campaign:

1 Follow up with KOLs to get key information that is only available to them.

It's important to follow up with influencers post-campaign, collect data and feedback and make changes for the future. On many Chinese social media platforms, performance data is private. Unless you're working with an influencer marketing platform that has tracking capabilities, you may have to get additional information from the influencer to measure the results of the campaign. For example, on Weibo, only the account holder can see the number of impressions a post received, and on many live streaming platforms, the total number of comments will only be shown to the streamer once the stream is complete.

2 Compare their results to their average post results as well as to the other influencers in the campaign.

This can tell you a lot about the effectiveness of the post and can also help weed out influencers who are buying fake engagements.

3 Give it time.

As mentioned previously, results don't appear immediately. Don't write off a campaign as a failure if you don't see an instant spike in traffic and sales. There tends to be a lag between influencer campaigns and increases in sales

4 Ask the influencer for honest feedback.

Brands rarely ask influencers to give them feedback, and that is truly a missed opportunity. For example, you could ask them how you could have better communicated the campaign brief, what they liked about the campaign, what was confusing or difficult about the campaign, what the overall sentiment of their audience was and what they would do differently if they could go back and do it again. This is incredibly valuable information that most influencers would be more than happy to share but are rarely asked.

5 Evaluate and Move On

After all the campaign results are in, brands should classify influencers according to their results and experiences. Those with poor content, who were difficult to work with, generated poor results or bought fake engagements should be allocated to a blacklist of people to avoid for future campaigns.

On the opposite end of the spectrum, those with above average results, who offered valuable feedback with healthy, professional work habits should be added to your roster of preferred influencers to work with again in the future.

Ongoing

Once the campaign is over, you may think that you're finished, but this is where you're wrong. Influencer marketing should be an ongoing effort or "always on". Of course, you'll need to run individual campaigns to promote events and product launches, but in between all of those your brand should still be collaborating and building relationships with influencers.

This is where many brands fail. They think of influencer marketing as individual campaign silos. They run one campaign and then disappear, not contacting the KOL again until the next campaign comes along. Brands should engage with KOLs and consumers all the time because building strong relationships with KOLs isn't a one-time effort.

And it's not just about building a rapport with KOLs. It's about constantly finding a way to get in front of your target audience.

A one-off campaign is like eating a candy bar for breakfast. It's a sugar high, creating a huge spike in searches and traffic. But it's temporary. Before you know it, the sugar high fades as consumers are inundated with messages about new products, and you're right back where you started — hungry and wondering why influencer marketing doesn't work.

"China and other markets have seen what I like to call "The Top-tier Influencer Death Spiral". The number of brands a top-tier influencer works with increases. Their engagement fee increases. Their connection with the brands they work with decreases and the quality and authenticity of their content decreases.

Because of this, I think we'll see more of a focus on micro-influencers. We're already starting to see a Moneyball approach to engaging micro-influencers – using data to ascertain which micro-influencers deliver high levels of engagement, in the most cost-effective manner."

— Michael Norris,
Consumer Research Manager at Resonance China

"Always on" campaigns are like a day full of healthy meals, creating sustainable energy that lasts and keeps you top of mind for consumers.

Brands should be working with 10 or more KOLs per month, even if it's simply product seeding. The more, the better.

7.3 KOL Relationship Management

When influencers love your products it shows. They go above and beyond and know they'll be rewarded with future projects. The more you work together, the smoother the working relationship becomes. This kind of relationship is extremely helpful when you need to execute crisis management or have other urgent needs or tight deadlines. You know you can get reliable results from someone you trust.

Long-term collaborations also mean that content is more authentic. This increases brand status and credibility.

Here are some best practices for KOL relationship management.

1 Be a fan

Study KOLs and their style and content before you contact them. Pay attention to the details and consume their content. Continue following them and try to meet with them face to face when possible. Brands want to work with influencers who are fans just as influencers want to work with brands who like their work.

2 Only approach relevant influencers

Relevance is the number one motivator for influencers. If your product and brand don't resonate with their audience, the content won't do well. In turn, neither of you will want to keep working together.

3 Regularly involve them in campaigns and stay in touch

Even if it's only for 2 campaigns a year, brands should stay in touch with influencers. The worst thing you can do after a campaign is disappear, leaving the influencer wondering if they'll ever hear from you again.

4 Give them creative freedom and ask for feedback

Reputable influencers put their audience first and don't want to put out any work that doesn't fit their style and range and they refuse to work with brands that are too controlling. Allowing them to have creative freedom in this regard not only enables a smoother working relationship but ensures a higher standard of content. Show that you value their opinion and ask for feedback and ideas.

5 Compensate them fairly

Nobody wants work with anyone they feel is taking advantage of them. Recognize an influencer's value and compensate them accordingly.

Although there might be some occasions when working with a micro-influencer may be done in exchange for an association with a brands, in China, even micro-influencers usually expect payment for formal campaigns.

This can be done in simple ways. Invite them to brand events, dinners or special events. They will be very interested in events where they can connect with other influencers or events that will help them create good content.

Gifting thoughtful, relevant brand products is an excellent way to maintain long-term relationships with influencers. This can also get you valuable feedback and possible free exposure via product seeding.

CHAPTER 8

Where Does It Go From Here?

KOLs Are Here to Stay

To kick off this chapter, we need to ask, is KOL marketing in China growing, stagnating or declining?

There's no doubt in our minds that influencer marketing will continue to grow and be a key component of a China marketing strategy. However, what influencer marketing looks like today is not what it'll look like in a year.

As Elaine Wong, founder of Double V Consulting explains, "The impact of influencers in the near future will stay the same, but the way they play the game will be different."

Even as formats and approaches change, the fundamentals behind the effectiveness of influencer marketing remain. The trust and the relationship an influencer has with his or her followers is the key.

Jeff Fish, co-founder of TMG Worldwide agrees, "I think the future of influencer marketing in China is strong. Trust will always be a factor in China marketing and if a KOL builds that trust with their respective audience there'll be a need in every vertical for their services. However, I do see a movement from just following a KOL to having much more meaningful access to them."

Thomas Graziani, co-founder of WalktheChat, doesn't see it as a matter of trust, but that influencers are simply the best option. "KOL marketing is definitely growing fast in China. The reason is that platforms have so far failed to deliver on the promise of efficient cost-per-click advertising. This left a wide space for KOLs to step-in and offer more personal and profitable marketing services," he says.

Right now, and for the foreseeable future, working with influencers is going to remain one of the best marketing methods in China. But brands need to take into account evolving attitudes and approaches when developing their influencer marketing strategy.

8.1   How Are Consumers' Attitudes Towards Influencers Changing?

Maturing Awareness

A May 2018 study from consulting firm A.T. Kearney showed that social media users in China are more open to recommendations by celebrities (78%) and micro-influencers / online celebrities (63%) than in any country surveyed. To get a sense of the gap, the US was ranked second at 38% and 49% respectively.

However, while Chinese consumers still trust high-quality influencers, they've become more critical of influencers who they feel are just trying to make a quick buck and are more knowledgeable about soft sell techniques.

Transparency, Authenticity and Soft Selling

As Graziani explains, "Consumers are more and more aware of native advertising and other types of soft marketing. As time goes by, KOLs are becoming more and more honest with their followers. For example, flagging sponsored posts is a growing trend. Readers like to know that influencers are communicating in a transparent way."

Food and beverage influencer Antoine Bunel agrees, explaining that Chinese consumers want advice from influencers, but they want assurances that the advice is real. "People have started to get used to seeing sponsored content. It's OK in China as people are willing to buy and be told what's good. I get asked a lot what kitchen equipment to buy. Though I've seen backlash on unsuitable channels where the sponsored post is different from the influencer's regular content."

Though the word has become a bit cliché, authenticity is what consumers are seeking. If it's obvious that the influencer does not and would not use the product they're promoting, there will be backlash. "Consumers know that influencers are compensated by the brands they represent so for there to be lasting engagement the influencer needs to prove that they really do use and value the brand or products they're promoting," says Fish.

"The audience is looking for condensed knowledge and urging KOLs to produce higher quality content, including long articles, pictures and videos. However, with the increasing number of bloggers online, I think in the future, audiences will be more interested in "real-life" bloggers who demonstrate their lifestyle to the audience. Watching someone else's life is interesting and inspirational."

— Susie Hu, Weibo and Bilibili blogger

Along these lines, Elaine Wong feels that to avoid rubbing consumers the wrong way, brands need to focus less on the hard sell. "Previously, direct selling used to work, however, in today's consumer environment, KOLs are more focused on soft selling. Brands will find sales will catch up gradually over time."

Soft selling and an authentic approach are particularly important when trying to reach young Millennial (Post-90s) and Gen Z (Post-00s) consumers, groups that brands are eager to reach.

Wong explained, "A brand's future in China is based on Millennials and Gen Z. These generations are becoming the biggest cluster of consumers in today's generation. They have grown up in the era of the internet and have access to all sorts of information and options in China as well as outside of China. This generation is massively influenced by their peers and have a strong desire to follow the current trends that are out there and that are always changing."

In surveys, young Chinese consumers claim that they don't value certain influencers, but this isn't necessarily true. Some studies have used terms that may be closer to "wanghong" than "trusted reviewer". China's Gen Z are also known for wanting to be more independent and have their own style and thoughts. They may not want to admit or maybe don't realize that they've been influenced by others. Some, for example, claim that their final purchasing decisions are theirs alone, based on their style and not influenced by KOLs. But at the same time, they admit that, when researching the product, they do look to see what KOLs have to say about it.

8.2   Difficulties Facing Content Creators in China

While the future is bright, there are definitely some difficulties facing both influencers and brands.

1 It's harder for influencers to stay independent

A growing number of platforms are partnering with multi-channel networks (MCNs) and becoming pay-to-play. A multi-channel network is an organization that works as a broker between platforms and influencers. They work for platforms or channel owners to arrange programming, funding, cross-promotion, partner management, digital rights management, monetization or audience development in exchange for a percentage of the revenue.

While there are numerous benefits to joining an MCN, such as increased promotion and growth opportunities and potentially more sponsorship opportunities, there are also a lot of downsides. Influencers are often lured to MCNs with the promise of brand deals. Unfortunately, these opportunities are limited to the relationships a particular network has and who the network steers a brand towards. Many MCNs also sign too many creators, which can be good for the network but can compromise the attention afforded to individual influencers. And the issues go on, from unfair contracts, to significant fees and more.

Live streaming platforms, Douyin, Xiaohongshu and other popular social media channels are carving up their user traffic and forming closer bonds with MCNs so, increasingly, influencers who wouldn't normally sign away their rights to an MCN have no choice but to do so. In this environment, new, independent creators will find it increasingly difficult to grow an audience on their own. But it's not only MCNs that are of concern.

Platforms such as Weibo are now so pay-to-play that it's nearly impossible to grow an audience from scratch without significant investment. Over the past couple of years, Weibo has dramatically reduced organic reach while simultaneously raising the cost for paid post promotion.

Weibo posted net revenues of 1.15 billion USD for the 2017 fiscal year, which was a 75% increase on the previous year. This was largely driven by surging advertising and marketing revenues which reached 996.7 million USD, up 75% year-on-year. This dramatic increase in revenue not only came from rising costs for brands, but for content creators as well.

2 Brands tend to work with same influencers, making it hard for new influencers to get their foot in the door

Journalist Jessica Rapp shared her thoughts. "The nature of one-to-one (not viral) social media platforms like WeChat and the fact that so many platforms are basically trying to get KOLs to sign contracts with them makes it a little difficult for new faces in the industry to really maintain a strong following for very long."

As mentioned above, MCNs are exacerbating the problem, making it difficult for new, independent creators to get traffic.

Furthermore, brands often like to play it safe, working with tried-and-true KOLs that have a track record of producing solid results for other brands. While this is understandable, it also means that brands typically recycle the same 1% of influencers over and over again, never giving the other 99% a chance.

This results in what Michael Norris refers to as the "Top-tier Influencer Death Spiral". As the number of brands a top-tier influencer works with increases, so do their fees. Meanwhile, their connection with the brands decreases, as does the quality and authenticity of their content.

In other words, many top-tier influencers have trouble balancing rising fame, increased commercial value and their original value proposition to followers, says Norris.

3 Fake it 'til you make it

While not isolated to influencers in China, many Chinese influencers have no problem 'faking it until they make it', expediting their way to the top by purchasing fake followers and engagements and building businesses on the backs of social media bots. These fake followers trick the public, and algorithms that choose which content to display, into believing they're more popular than they really are.

Influencers know that if they can get into the top rankings, agencies and brands will break down the door to work with them. However, there's a flaw in the system. Influencers can easily buy their way into the rankings by purchasing fake fans and engagements, which we know is a common practice in China, or by having an inside connection at the company creating the list. Furthermore, many agencies aren't actually vetting the influencers to find out if their following and engagement is fake or not.

These practices are so common in China, it makes it difficult for influencers who want to work with real engagements and fans only.

4 KOLs are exhausted by the constant need to evolve

KOLs understand that it's important to stay on top of new trends and follow consumer attention, but in China that can be extremely difficult as trends change at a faster pace than anywhere else in the world.

As mentioned earlier in the book, coming out of seemingly nowhere, starting in later 2015 live streaming became extremely popular in China, every brand, agency, influencer, and those hoping to become influencers jumped on the streaming bandwagon. All marketing strategies shifted to include streaming. Then only two years later came the rise of short video and WeChat mini programs.

For influencers, this constant need to evolve and try new platforms and content types while maintaining their core following can be exhausting. It's hard to know which platforms will take off, and which ones will end up being a waste of time.

Though it's a gamble, waiting too long can mean missing out. Those who jumped on Douyin in its early days were in prime position when the platform's user numbers exploded in early 2018.

5 Influencer incubators are now big players

Behind many of these huge bloggers and their online stores are companies known as blogger incubators. They're e-commerce companies that, instead of creating stores and hiring bloggers to promote them, flip the model on its head.

First, they create marketing channels and a customer base by developing bloggers with massive, loyal followings. Then they create the products. Blogger incubators are like traditional talent agencies except that the source of income is not advertising commissions but sales revenue from individual bloggers' online stores.

Each blogger the incubator works with has their own following, their own store, and their own self-branded products. To the average consumer, it appears these bloggers all work independently. It's nearly impossible to tell that they're working with an incubator.

Jessica Rapp, senior writer at Jing Daily, outlines some of her concerns surrounding the phenomenon of KOL incubators, or as she calls them, KOL factories.

"There's always talk that the "bubble will burst," especially now that much of the KOL management has been taken over by KOL factories. These agencies train tens of thousands of KOLs that all have supposedly huge fan bases. It seems unlikely that a structure like that can really produce influencers that will establish lasting trust and connections with their followers in the long run," explained Jessica.

"People are likely to get tired of what will no doubt eventually be perceived as a lack of authenticity, save for the few who can really produce genuine, quality content that's, at least seemingly, organic and true to their lifestyle and their own talent, not dependent on the brands they endorse. You're already starting to see this pattern in the beauty market in the West – Instagram accounts like "gelcream" and "chemist.confessions" that claim to not work with brands, instead just giving their genuine opinions and thoughts about products."

8.3   Trends

Marketers and brands must remember, China's culture and economy are developing more rapidly than you can imagine. And that heavily affects Chinese social media and consumer behavior. Platforms come and go, new content trends emerge and disappear and top influencers rise and fall all in the blink of an eye.

Influencers will adapt as platforms and content types change, but their role as thought and community leaders will remain.

Here are some platform and content trends that we see coming.

1 Increased fragmentation

"Influencer marketing has been evolving fast in China. What started as campaigns on big Weibo and WeChat accounts is now expanding in scope. More platforms are involved, from Q&A platforms like Zhihu to short-video platforms like Douyin. Moreover, influencers are no longer just massive accounts. A combination of bigger and smaller accounts is increasingly becoming the go-to strategy for many brands with ambitious KOL plans.

It's likely that platforms will try to empower brands to user smaller KOLs through more automated systems inside the platforms themselves. This will enable WeChat, Weibo and the other platforms to also get a cut of the advertising spend. Cost-per-click will also become more mature, and will compete for budget with influencer marketing, which might ultimately contain the increase of KOL prices." says Thomas Graziani.

2 The rise of the micro-KOL

Micro-KOLs are attractive to younger consumers who see themselves as more independent and less prone to the influence of commercial interests and personalities. Brands are attracted to them because they have specific niche audiences. They're also much more accessible for brands with modest budgets, are seen as more authentic and have greater engagement with their audience.

According to Michael Norris, "Faced with skyrocketing influencer marketing costs and increased indifference to overly-commercialised top-tier influencers, brands will turn to more cost-effective micro-influencers. Importantly, micro-influencers also have the advantage of being closer to their communities and are, at least for the moment, immune from the 'influencer death spiral' which increased exposure and commercial success can bring.

We're already starting to see a Moneyball approach to engaging micro-influencers – using data to ascertain which micro-influencers deliver high levels of engagement, in the most cost-effective manner. This approach will continue to evolve, but reinforces how sensitive brands are becoming to higher influencer marketing costs."

Does this mean brands should ditch large KOLs and only engage with micro KOLs? No. As Jeff Fish puts it, "Don't just go after the big KOL. Make sure there is a mix of micro-KOLs, traditional paid media, O2O and experiential marketing in every campaign."

A combination of top, mid-tier, and micro-KOLs is often best for a campaign to achieve the greatest effect.

3 Influencer-run WeChat mini program e-commerce stores are on the rise

A growing number of WeChat influencers are launching stores. Influencers that can wield this kind of power will become the most sought after. A report by Michael Norris predicts that WeChat mini program stores will become one of the top online channels for luxury products in the near future. Agencies that create these mini stores have also popped up to fill this need in the market.

While some influencers like Becky Li are starting their own brands, others like Gogoboi and Annystyleontop curate goods from luxury e-commerce retailers like Yoox, Net-A-Porter, and Farfetch.

Popular fashion blogger Mr. Bags has gone another route. His WeChat mini program store is limited to exclusive capsule collections that he co-designs with top luxury brands including TOD's and Longchamp. Many of these collections have sold out in in minutes.

4 Weibo is expensive but still necessary

Weibo and WeChat are the bread and butter of Chinese social media platforms. Similar to Instagram and Facebook in the West, they're the mature, proven, go-to platforms.

Although Weibo is no longer in the limelight, it remains a powerful tool for users and advertisers alike. Competition is growing, but continued innovation from Weibo will likely enable the network to stay on top of its niche for a while.

It's important to note however, that Weibo is becoming increasingly expensive, monetizing the success of KOL marketing by charging brands a fee to run sponsored posts.

While Weibo is able to get away with charging those fees right now, as other social media platforms emerge, brands and KOLs may slowly shift to less expensive and less restrictive platforms.

5 Short video – extremely popular, but not for all brands

As Fabian Bern, founder and managing director of marketing firm Uplab, puts it, "We see a growing trend in video and I believe this will grow in the coming years significantly. Platforms will integrate easier and more accessible ways for brands to advertise, whether it's through influencers or not."

Short video has become extremely popular in China in 2018, and while some are finding great success, others are far from achieving any kind of worthwhile ROI.

While we definitely encourage experimentation, brands also need to carefully consider if this medium is a good fit.

6 Live streaming

While many brands have rushed to short video, live streaming is still a very relevant and powerful way to reach your audience. It can be used for e-commerce, event broadcasting and branded programming. Travel and experiential brands have yet to really use live streaming to its full potential and there are lots of opportunities there. E-sports are also on the rise and there are plenty of sponsorship opportunities there.

7 Social commerce

Social media and e-commerce have always been interconnected in China but now we're seeing that to a greater degree. "KOLs have huge selling power on social media platforms so I think e-commerce social media and technology companies are going to try to figure out how to best benefit from this model so that they don't lose out," says Jessica Rapp.

"For example, e-commerce giants are all launching their own creative content platforms, like Douyin, so that they can produce more sales through short video endorsements. It also seems that, though this may be a stretch, given the rise of social commerce, spreading the word about products by reaching smaller micro-influencers who in turn influence groups of friends, a model expertly harnessed by new apps like Pinduoduo, is going to be increasingly key."

Antoine Bunel feels that some large rivalries will have major effects. "With Alibaba and Tencent at war, there will be more acquisitions and evolutions. I'm sure Tencent will come up with better integrations of video within WeChat. And I expect better search and e-commerce in WeChat too. Alibaba has a crazy strong ecosystem and its partnership with Toutiao will be big, I'm also expecting new types of KOL entertainment, linked with Youku."

8 An increasing presence of Western influencers

Kim Kardashian opened an account on Xiaohongshu in October 2018. She is just one of many international celebrities who have been and will continue to open accounts on major Chinese social media and social e-commerce platforms. For many celebrities, they want a more direct connection with their Chinese fans. For more commercially oriented figures with brands and lines of their own, China's huge consumer market beckons.

9 The changing role of the influencer

We will see influencers taking on additional roles to utilize their expertise, such as:

- Influencers as agencies
- Influencers as consultants, brand advisors

- Influencers as co-designers

- Influencers with their own brands

- Influencers taking more control

So there you have it. Key opinion leaders are powerful, effective marketing allies and they're definitely here to stay. As the scene develops, some are becoming even more powerful. You can't escape them so start early, build relationships with them and put your new knowledge to work. This will put you at the forefront and ahead of your competitors when the next wave of change arrives.

Acknowledgements

This book has been a team effort and we're grateful to the many people who have helped us make it a reality. First and foremost a big thank you goes to the wonderful Alarice team that contributed writing, research, design and their many talents: Sammi Wong, Jackie Chan, Jacqueline Chan, Flora Lin, Natalia Drachuk, Mason Ku and Eric Tse.

To our fantastic editor Maureen Lea, who made the book flow. :)

To our spouses Marius and Hank, for always being there for us, no matter what we're doing.

With special thanks to:

Elijah Whaley

Becky Li

Thomas Graziani

Michael Norris

Antoine Bunel

Jeff Fish

Yi Li

Elaine Wong

Susie Hu

Fabian Bern

Jessica Rapp

Appendix

1. China's Social Media Landscape

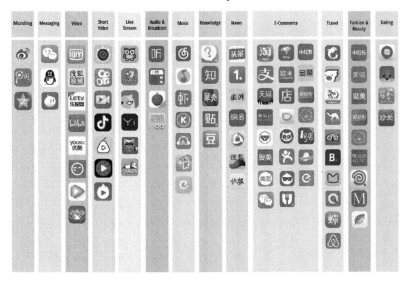

Common Chinese social media platforms listed by function.

Microblogs	Weibo, Qzone
Messaging	Wechat, QQ, Aliwangwang
Video	iQiyi, Sohu TV, LeTV, Bilibili, Youku, Tudou, Tencent Video, Acfun
Short video	Miaopai, Kuaishou, Meipai, Douyin, Pear Video, Watermelon TV, Hypstar
Live streaming	Inke, Douyu, Huajiao, Yizhibo, YY TV, PandaTV
Audio and Broadcasting	Ximalaya FM, Qingting FM, Lizhi FM
Music	Netease Music, QQ Music, Xiami Music, Kuguo music, Kuwo Music

Knowledge	Zhihu, Guoke, Baidu Tieba, Baidu Zhidao
News	Toutiao, YiDian, PengPai, NetEase, Tencent News, Sohu News, Kuaibao
E-commerce	Taobao, JD.com, Xiaohongshu, Alipay, Nuomi, Xianyu, Tmall, Wei shop, Mogu Street, VIP shop, Meilishuo, Kaola, Maoyan, Yihao shop, Jumei, Dianping, Meituan, Taopiaopiao, ele.me, WeChat
Travel	Ctrip, FlyingPig, Qunar, Didi Chuxing, TripAdvisor, Booking.com, Mafengwo, Qyer, Chan Travel, Airbnb
Fashion and Beauty	Xiaohongshu, Meila, Jumei, Mogu Street, Meilishuo, Vipshop
Dating	Momo, Tantan, Baihe, Zhenai

2. Marketing Strategies for WeChat and Weibo

	WeChat	Weibo
Increase exposure	Interactive H5 KOL promotion UGC + incentives Unique content	Intensive ads KOL promotion Creative video Live streaming
Increase sales	WeChat ads KOL crossover Exclusive coupons + discounts	Campaigns +Weibo Window KOL promotion codes KOL trials Live streaming with "Watch and Buy"
Increase followers	Lucky draws UGC + incenitves KOL poromotion	Lucky draw UGC + incentives KOL live streaming

3. List of KOL Agencies

Name	Website	Services	Platforms
Antipodal Talent	www.antipodal.com	KOL and internet celebrity talent management, KOL marketing strategy, KOL live streaming campaign management	Weibo, WeChat, Yizhibo, Huajiao, Inke, Miaopai, Taobao, Tencent TV etc.
AsiaKOL	www.asiakol.com	KOL research, KOL management, KOL marketing campaigns, KOL marketing strategy, KOl databases	Weibo, WeChat, Meipai, Yizhibo and other live streaming platforms
Gushan Culture	www.weibo.com/3877848191	KOL management	Weibo and WeChat
iconKOL	www.iconkol.com	KOL search, customized KOL marketing campaigns, KOl databases	
KOLSTORE	www.kolstore.com	KOL search, KOL databases	WeChat and Weibo
Louis Communication	www.loushijt.com	KOL management	Weibo, WeChat, Meipai
PRAD	www.myprad.com	KOL search, KOL contact, KOL databases	WeChat, Inke, Huajiao, Yizhibo
PARKLU	www.parklu.com	KOL research, KOL campaign management, KOL content strategy, KOL databases, brand ambassador recruitment and management, top and mid-tier KOL engagement, KOL network coverage for Mainland China, Hong Kong and overseas Chinese	WeChat, Weibo, Youku, Meipai, Yizhibo, Inke, Xiaohongshu, Meilimeizhuang, Instagram

Viral Access	www.viralaccess.asia	Marketing, social media, digital marketing, branding, KOL management, Micro-KOL marketing strategy	Weibo, Instagram, Facebook, YouTube
Weiboyi	www.weiboyi.com	KOL campaigns	Weibo, WeChat, QQ

4. Some Prominent KOLs Mentioned in this Book

Papi Jiang / Jiang Yilei
Weibo: papi酱
www.weibo.com/xiaopapi
Youku: i.youku.com/papijiang
Youtube:
www.youtube.com/channel/UCgHXsynhD8GxbFcNl
PEn-_w

Mr. Bags
Weibo: Bags包先生
www.weibo.com/bagszhuyejunlt
WeChat: bagsbaoxiansheng

Becky Li / Li Beika / Becky's Fantasy
WeChat: Miss_shopping_li

Thomas Ye Si
Weibo: gogoboi
www.weibo.com/gogoboi
WeChat: realgogoboi
Youku: i.youku.com/gogoboi

Dipsy
Weibo: Dipsy迪西
www.weibo.com/houzimi
WeChat: realDipsy

Anna
Weibo: onlyanna
www.weibo.com/u/1736315592
Taobao store: Anna It Is Amazing (aka ASM)
https://onlyanna.world.taobao.com

Cherie / 朱宸慧
Weibo: 雪梨Cherie
www.weibo.com/zhuhuihui28

Zhang Dayi
Weibo: 张大奕eve
www.weibo.com/zhangyieve
Taobao Store: 吾欢喜的衣橱
https://bigeve8.world.taobao.com

5. KOL Recommendations by Industry

Mainstream celebrities are not included in this list.

ID	FOLLOWERS	WEIBO LINK
General		
回忆专用小马甲 (Hui Yi Zhuang Yong Xiao Ma Jia)	32.4 million	http://weibo.com/p/1005053217179555
同道大叔 (Tong Dao Da Shu)	15.9 million	http://weibo.com/tongdaodashu

papi酱 (Papi Jiang)	28.8 million	http://weibo.com/xiaopapi
叫兽易小星 (Jiao Shou Yi Xiao Xing)	8.7 million	http://weibo.com/jiaoshoutv
天才小熊猫 (Tian Cai Xiao Xiong Mao)	7.1 million	http://weibo.com/panada
Fashion & Beauty		
徐峰立 (Peter Xu Fengli)	7.4 million	http://weibo.com/u/1617902267
gogoboi	9 million	http://weibo.com/gogoboi
Chrison克里森	6.5 million	http://weibo.com/modiac
Dipsy迪西	6.1 million	http://weibo.com/houzimi
FashionModels	6.8 million	http://weibo.com/fashiononion
IT & Digital		
互联网的那点事 (Hu Lian Wang De Na Dian Shi)	4.3 million	http://weibo.com/alibuybuy
数字尾巴 (DGtle)	5.1 million	http://weibo.com/dgtle
IT大施兄 (IT Da Shi Xiong)	754,000	http://weibo.com/ixap
魏布斯 (Wei Bu Si)	746,000	http://weibo.com/weibusi
月光博客 (Yue Guang Blog)	679,000	http://weibo.com/williamlong
Travel & Hospitality		
美少女颜究所 (Mei Shao Nu Yan Jiu Suo)	3.9 million	http://weibo.com/u/1934303255
365个旅行攻略 (365 Ge Lu Xing Gong Lue)	6.6 million	http://weibo.com/u/2936882141
我的旅行小马甲 (Wo De Lu Xing Xiao Ma Jia)	3.7 million	http://www.weibo.com/p/1005052025994775
猫力molly	4.9 million	http://weibo.com/smilemolly

Food & Beverage		
Nicole的生活书 (Nicole De Sheng Huo Shu)	3.3 million	http://www.weibo.com/nicole831026
文怡 (Wen Yi)	5.4 million	http://weibo.com/wenyi
日食记 (Ri Shi Ji)	16.2 million	http://www.weibo.com/rishiji
我与美食的日常 (Wo Yu Mei Shi De Ri Chang)	4.3 million	http://weibo.com/u/5101863971
999道私房菜 (999 Dao Si Fang Cai)	15.4 million	http://weibo.com/u/2697416452

6. Zhihu KOLs

This link on Zhihu itself has a list of Zhihu KOLs. Site in Chinese.
https://www.zhihu.com/question/40599843

7. KOL Cost Estimation Tool

To understand average impressions, CPMs for Chinese social media platforms and campaign budgets, China influencer marketing platform PARKLU has an online estimator at http://app.parklu.com/calculator.

8. Campaign Ideas

Q&A

- How much do you know about our brand? [Question] [Read the content/watch the video/visit the website] to find out. Then repost this with your answer for a chance to win a prize.

- Summer has arrived! What's your must-have product this summer? Repost with your answer for a chance to win a prize.

- Guess who our new brand ambassador in China is? Repost this with his/her name. The answer will be announced on [date]. Those with correct answers get a chance to win [list of prizes].

- Our [number] year anniversary is coming! Help us celebrate. Repost with your wishes, comments or suggestions for a chance to win [list of prizes].

- Estimate how many [name of product]s we sell on average each day. Repost with your guess. Those with answers closest to the correct number get a chance to win [list of prizes]!

- [Question]? Do you know the answer? Pick A, B or C and repost this with your answer for a chance to win [list of prizes].

- Want to try our new product before we open sales to the public? Repost this and tell us why you should be selected. We'll pick [number of winners] lucky people for our free trial.

Game / Test

- Repost the riddles with your answers. Those who answer correctly will get the chance to win [list of prizes].

- Can you spot the differences between the two pictures? (*Post 2 slightly altered product images) Repost a picture with the differences circled. If you're right, you'll get the chance to win [list of prizes].

- Take our trivia test and repost it with your results for a chance to win [list of prizes].

- Can you read the secret words? (*Add words in Morse code or hidden in a picture) Repost with your answer for a chance to win [list of prizes].

- What's your [mantra/ lucky number/ travel destination] this month? Repost this with your screenshot for your chance to win [list of prizes].

(*This post requires a fast-changing GIF with different phrases, numbers etc. that users take a screenshot of to reveal their results.)

Hot Topic

- Which [football team/basketball team/tennis player] are you a fan of? Repost this with their name for a chance to win [list of prizes].

- Have you seen [TV drama/movie]? Which character is your favourite? Repost this with their name and your reason for a chance to win [list of prizes].

- The new year is coming! Repost this with 3 wishes for the coming year. We'll pick [number] lucky winners to receive our gift packages!

- Where's your dream holiday? Repost with your answer and reason for a chance to win [list of prizes].

- Do you want to say a big, warm "Thank you!" to your mom? Repost this for your chance to win [list of prizes] for Mothers' Day.

020

- Want to get an 80% discount in our offline store? Follow us and repost [certain content]. We'll pick [number] lucky winners to receive our special offer.

- Have you seen our posters [on the bus/ in the MTR station/at the airport]? Take a photo with one and repost it for a chance to win [list of prizes].

Bibliography

1.   Pan, Y. (June 14, 2017). How These 10 New KOL 'Rules' on Weibo Could Affect Luxury Brands in China. Retrieved September 24, 2018, from https://jingdaily.com/10-new-kols-rules-weibo-luxury-brands/

2.   Weibo Corporation. (November 7, 2017). Weibo Reports Third Quarter 2017 Financial Results. Retrieved September 28, 2018, from https://www.prnewswire.com/news-releases/weibo-reports-third-quarter-2017-financial-results-300550754.html

3.   Sina Weibo. (November 16, 2015). Weibo Community Regulations. Retrieved September 20, 2018, from http://www.liqucn.com/article/530949.shtml

4.   Digital Business Lab. (June 1, 2018). 5 Facts of China's Post-00's Generation's Consumption Habits. Retrieved September 20, 2018, from https://digital-business-lab.com/2018/06/post-00s-generations-consumption-habits/

5.   South China Morning Post. (June 14, 2017). China's new graduates earn US$588 a month ... less than the cost of an iPhone. Retrieved September 24, 2018, from https://www.scmp.com/news/china/society/article/2098225/chinas-new-graduates-earn-us588-month-less-cost-iphone

6.   World Economic Forum. (April 13, 2017). China now produces twice as many graduates a year as the US. Retrieved October 19, 2018, from https://www.weforum.org/agenda/2017/04/higher-education-in-china-has-boomed-in-the-last-decade

7.   Yangzi Sima and Peter C. Pugsley. (March 2010). The Rise of A 'Me Culture' in Postsocialist China: Youth, Individualism and Identity Creation in the Blogosphere. Retrieved October 21, 2018, from https://www.researchgate.net/publication/236876228_The_Rise_of_A_%27Me_Culture%27_in_Postsocialist_China_Youth_Individualism_and_Identity_Creation_in_the_Blogosphere

8.   Xiong, J. (December 4, 2017). Why Z-lennials Will Upend Western Brands' China Strategy. Retrieved September 14, 2018, from https://jingdaily.com/incoming-challenges-brands-chinese-z-lennials-generation-consumers/

9.   Joseph Pisani. (January 9, 2017). De Beers CEO Talks Diamonds and Millennial Marketing. Retrieved September 14, 2018, from https://www.thediamondloupe.com/articles/2017-01-09/de-beers-ceo-talks-diamonds-and-millennial-marketing

10. Harvard Business Review. (May 8, 2012). Catering to the Self-Expressive Chinese Consumer. Retrieved September 11, 2018, from https://hbr.org/2012/05/the-self-expressive-chinese-co

11. Rapp, J. (February 28, 2018). Brand Visibility Remains a Real Challenge on WeChat. Retrieved October 11, 2018, from https://jingdaily.com/brand-visibility-wechat/

12. Hallanan, L. (July 27, 2017). China Video KOLs Favor Authenticity Over Production Quality. Retrieved September 21, 2018, from https://www.parklu.com/china-video-kols-authenticity-quality/

13. South China Morning Post. (June 17, 2018). 5 Facts about spending and social habits of China's Post-00's generation. Retrieved October 20, 2018, from https://www.scmp.com/magazines/style/news-trends/article/2150711/5-facts-about-spending-and-social-habits-chinas-post-00s

14. Schawbel, D. (January 20, 2015). 10 New Findings About The Millennial Consumer. Retrieved October 15, 2018, from https://www.forbes.com/sites/danschawbel/2015/01/20/10-new-findings-about-the-millennial-consumer/#28f603516c8f

15. Hallanan, L. (February 22, 2018). The Life of a KOL: Running a Mini Influencer Marketing Agency. Retrieved October 15, 2018, from https://www.parklu.com/kol-mini-influencer-marketing-agency/

16. Hallanan, L. (March 22, 2018). Tactics China Wang Hong Use to Connect with Fans. Retrieved October 12, 2018, from https://www.parklu.com/tactics-china-wang-hong-fans/

17. Pan, Y. (April 19, 2018). The Devil WeChats About Prada — The Threat of China's Celebrity Fashion Editors. Retrieved October 6, 2018, from https://jingdaily.com/fashion-editors/

18. Zheng, R. (February 7, 2018). The 10 Most Influential Fashion Stylists in China. Retrieved September 6, 2018, from https://jingdaily.com/top-10-fashion-stylists-in-china/

19. Hallanan, L. (June 21, 2018). Weitao KOLs Reinvent Taobao & Tmall Social Commerce. Retrieved October 16, 2018, from http://www.parklu.com/category/china-social-networks/weitao/

20. Hallanan, L. (November 24, 2017). China Influencer Brands Crush 11.11 Singles Day Sales. Retrieved September 1, 2018, from https://www.parklu.com/china-influencer-brands-11-11-singles-day-sales/

21. Hallanan, L. (December 29, 2017). Wechat Mini-Programs Revolutionize KOL Sales Campaigns. Retrieved September 13, 2018, from https://www.parklu.com/wechat-mini-programs-kol-sales-campaigns/

22. Zheng, R. (July 19, 2017). Givenchy Wins on Gogoboi's New E-Commerce Channel. Retrieved October 4, 2018, from https://jingdaily.com/givenchy-becomes-first-luxury-brand-sell-gogobois-e-commerce-channel/

23. Rapp, J. (December 1, 2017). WeChat Star Becky Li Goes Back to Basics in New Fashion Line. Retrieved October 8, 2018, from https://jingdaily.com/wechat-fashion-star-becky-li-bringing-back-basics/

24. Halliday, S. (June 26, 2018). Tod's is first luxe label to premiere a product with a blogger on WeChat Mini. Retrieved September 7, 2018, from http://us.fashionnetwork.com/news/Tod-s-is-first-luxe-label-to-premiere-a-product-with-a-blogger-on-WeChat-Mini,991579.html#.W7csHhRoTQp

25. Ap, T. (June 11, 2018). Mr. Bags Designs Tod's Purse for WeChat 'Baoshop' Launch. Retrieved August 27, 2018, from https://wwd.com/fashion-news/fashion-scoops/mr-bags-designs-tods-purse-for-wechat-baoshop-launch-1202702927/

26. Doland, A. (February 11, 2018). China's Influencers Don't Just Push Brands -- They Create Their Own. Retrieved October 17, 2018, from http://adage.com/article/digital/china-s-influencers-create-brands/312229/

27. Contestabile, G. (January 15, 2018) Influencer Marketing in 2018: Becoming an Efficient Marketplace. Retrieved October 15, 2018, from https://www.adweek.com/digital/giordano-contestabile-activate-by-bloglovin-guest-post-influencer-marketing-in-2018/

28. Hallanan, L. (April 26, 2018). 3 Most Important Resources for KOL Marketing in China in 2018. Retrieved October 16, 2018, from https://www.parklu.com/kol-marketing-china-2018/

29. Pan, Y. (July 22, 2018). Dior's Pushy Relaunch of Iconic Bag Backfires in China. Retrieved October 13, 2018, from https://jingdaily.com/dior-saddle-bag-china/

30. Hallanan, L. (May 18, 2018). Budgeting for Digital Marketing in China, Explained. Retrieved October 10, 2018, from https://jingdaily.com/budgeting-digital-marketing-china/

31. Hallanan, L. (May 3, 2018). An "Always-On" KOL Marketing Strategy Beats Out One-Off Campaigns. Retrieved October 6, 2018, from https://www.parklu.com/kol-marketing-strategy-campaigns/

32.   Hallanan, L. (May 17, 2018). Your China Market Entry Strategy & KOL Marketing Challenges. Retrieved October 6, 2018, from https://www.parklu.com/china-market-entry-strategy-kol-marketing-challenges/

33.   Chen, Y. (June 10, 2018). Xiaohongshu (Little Red Book) is fostering e-commerce via word of mouth. Retrieved September 6, 2018, from https://walkthechat.com/xiaohongshu-little-red-book-fostering-e-commerce-via-word-mouth/

34.   Westwin. (n.d.) 2018 Research Report On Chinese Consumer Cross-Border Purchasing Behavior. Retrieved October 6, 2018, from https://adstochina.westwin.com/China_Cross-border_Consumption_report_en.pdf

35.   Hallanan, L. (June 21, 2018). Weitao KOLs Reinvent Taobao & Tmall Social Commerce. Retrieved September 16, 2018, from https://www.parklu.com/weitao-kols-taobao-tmall-social-commerce/

36.   Frost & Sullivan, The Cross-Border E-Commerce Opportunity In China. Preview only retrieved October 6, 2018 from https://www.azoyagroup.com/resources/view/the-cross-border-e-commerce-opportunity-in-china-frost-sullivan-preview/

37.   Angela Doland. (March 17, 2016). Half of China's Ad Spending Will Go Toward the Internet This Year, GroupM Says The Flipside: Spending on TV is Expected to Drop 4.5% in 2016. Retrieved October 21, 2018, from http://adage.com/article/digital/half-c/303175/

38.   Perez, B. (March 8, 2017). Alibaba, Baidu, Tencent dominate China's red-hot digital advertising market. Retrieved September 16, 2018, from https://www.scmp.com/tech/china-tech/article/2076802/alibaba-baidu-tencent-dominate-chinas-red-hot-digital-advertising

39.   Griffiths, T. (October 20, 2016). WeChat Improves Advert Targeting with Hyper-local Moments Ads. Retrieved September 17, 2018, from https://www.linkedin.com/pulse/wechat-improves-advert-targeting-hyper-local-moments-ads-griffiths/?trk=prof-post

40.   Gao, C. (n.d.). 5 Trends for Chinese Social Media Marketing in 2018. Retrieved October 17, 2018, from http://www.theegg.com/social/china/chinese-social-media-marketing-trends-2018/

41.   Whaley, E. (May 9, 2018). Gucci, Chanel, and Dior Lead on Chinese Social Media: PARKLU Report. Retrieved October 16, 2018, from https://jingdaily.com/chinese-social-media-parklu/

42.   Hallanan, L. (April 24, 2018). The 3 Problems Ruining Brand-Agency Relationships in China. Retrieved September 6, 2018, from https://jingdaily.com/problems-ruining-brand-agency/

43.   Cheung, A. (September 15, 2015). Courting Chinese Consumers: Winning brands are keeping it personal. Retrieved September 6, 2018, from https://www.elmwood.com/thoughts/courting-chinese-consumers/

44.   Tencent. (August 15, 2018). 腾讯公布2018年第二季度及中期. Retrieved October 16, 2018, from https://www.tencent.com/zh-cn/articles/8003521534381984.pdf

45.   WeChat Chatterbox. (November 9, 2017).The 2017 WeChat Data Report. Retrieved September 16, 2018, from https://blog.wechat.com/2017/11/09/the-2017-wechat-data-report/

46.   China Academy of Information and Communications Technology Industry and Planning Research Institute. (April 2018). Build an Innovative Community of Shared Ecosystem and Foster New Drivers of Economic Growth - WeChat Economic and Social Impact Report 2017. Retrieved October 21, 2018, from http://www.caict.ac.cn/kxyj/qwfb/ztbg/201805/P020180529380481819634.pdf

47.   Sina Weibo. (August 08, 2018). 博发布2018年第二季度未经审计财报 Weibo releases its unaudited financial reports for Q2 2018 https://tech.sina.com.cn/i/2018-08-08/doc-ihhkuskt9159883.shtml

48.   Weibo. (December 25, 2017). 2017微博用户发展报告 2017 Weibo User Development Report. Retrieved October 21, 2018, from http://data.weibo.com/report/reportDetail?id=404

49.   Wang Zhongxin Ai Wei. (February 6, 2018). 蚂蜂窝"更名为"马蜂窝. Retrieved October 22, 2018, from http://www.bjnews.com.cn/travel/2018/02/06/475443.html

50.   Mafengwo Travel News. (February 26, 2018). 马蜂窝进化论：从新潮旅行社区到国民旅游品牌 - 马蜂窝. Retrieved October 22, 2018, from http://www.mafengwo.cn/travel-news/1424122.html

51.   China Internet Network Information Center. (July, 2018). 中国互联网络发展状况统计报告 Statistical Report on the Development of China's Internet. Retrieved October 22, 2018, from http://www.cnnic.net.cn/gywm/xwzx/rdxw/20172017_7047/201808/P020180820603445431468.pdf

52.   Baidu staff. (March 26, 2018). 抖音短视频KOL营销5大内容玩法. Retrieved October 22, 2018, from https://baijiahao.baidu.com/s?id=1595983729330400831&wfr=spider&for=pc

53.   Iimedia. (May 28, 2018). 2018Q1中国在线直播行业研究报告. Retrieved October 9, 2018, from http://www.iimedia.cn/61402.html

54.   Majia. (February 27, 2018). 淘宝直播"上位"：日销售额过亿，有些商家已经赚翻. Retrieved October 19, 2018, from http://www.maijia.com/news/article/440904

55. Sohu. (June 12, 2018). 划! 重! 点! 解读小红书"明星+KOL"的爆款法则. Retrieved October 19, 2018, from https://www.sohu.com/a/235322920_378903

56. Zheng, R. (May 13, 2018). How Chinese Consumers Engage With Luxury Livestreamers. Retrieved October 10, 2018, from https://jingdaily.com/luxury-livestream/

57. Hallanan, L. (July 11, 2018). CIM Episode 028: Why Ecommerce Live Streaming is the Future of Retail with Liyia Wu, Founder and CEO of ShopShops. Retrieved October 5, 2018, from http://www.chinainfluencermarketing.com/2018/07/cim028/

58. Bobila, M. (July 19, 2017). Meet ShopShops, An Interactive, Online Retail Experience For Fashion-Savvy Chinese Consumers. Retrieved September 25, 2018, from https://fashionista.com/2017/07/shop-shops-chinese-app

59. Pan, Y. (June 16, 2017). Chinese Startup Gets Over $4 Million to Help KOLs Run Their Business. Retrieved September 14, 2018, from https://jingdaily.com/chinese-startup-look-helps-kols-run-business/

60. Hallanan, L. (December 29, 2017). Wechat Mini-Programs Revolutionize KOL Sales Campaigns. Retrieved September 24, 2018, from https://www.parklu.com/wechat-mini-programs-kol-sales-campaigns/

61. Hallanan, L. (June 13, 2018). Why China's Viral Video App Douyin is No Good for Luxury. Retrieved September 24, 2018, from https://jingdaily.com/douyin-not-for-luxury-brands/

62. Linkfluence. (May 23, 2018). Douyin (Tik Tok) has taken Asia by Storm - Can it Last? Retrieved October 16, 2018, from https://linkfluence.com/douyin-tik-tok-has-taken-asia-by-storm-can-it-last/

63. Graziana, T. (July 30, 2018). How Douyin became China's top short-video App in 500 days. Retrieved September 12, 2018, from https://walkthechat.com/douyin-became-chinas-top-short-video-app-500-days/

64. 茉小莉. (April 2, 2018). 抖音、AI、3D打印，我们找到了「答案茶」爆红的真相. Retrieved September 4, 2018, from https://36kr.com/p/5125901.html

65. Sohu. (April 30, 2018). 抖音网红答案茶为什么突然就火了 原因竟然出在"占卜"! Retrieved October 4, 2018, from http://www.sohu.com/a/229912724_712513

66. Technode. (June 13, 2018). Xiaohongshu is fostering e-commerce via word of mouth. Retrieved September 3, 2018, from https://technode.com/2018/06/13/xiaohongshu/

67. China Internet Watch. (July 9, 2018). Cross-border e-commerce startup Xiaohongshu reached 100 mn users in May 2018. Retrieved October 5, 2018, from https://www.chinainternetwatch.com/25198/xiaohongshu-may-2018/

68. CNBC. (September 18, 2018). The biggest trend in Chinese social media is dying, and another has already taken its place. Retrieved October 6, 2018, from https://www.cnbc.com/2018/09/19/short-video-apps-like-douyin-tiktok-are-dominating-chinese-screens.html

69. Cheung, M. (May 2, 2018). Why Marketers In China Are Tapping into Short Video Apps. Retrieved October 8, 2018, from https://www.emarketer.com/content/china-s-marketers-pay-close-attention-to-the-short-video-apps-douyin-and-kuaishou

70. Zhu, L. (July 17, 2018). Douyin records 500 million global monthly active users. Retrieved September 18, 2018, from http://www.chinadaily.com.cn/a/201807/17/WS5b4d6057a310796df4df6e3c.html

71. Liu, J. (July 17, 2018). Douyin reaches 500 million monthly active users worldwide. Retrieved October 11, 2018, from https://technode.com/2018/07/17/douyin-500-million-mau/

72. South China Morning Post. (June 13, 2018). Most downloaded iPhone app Tik Tok hits 150 million daily users in China, marking major milestone. Retrieved October 18, 2018, from https://www.scmp.com/tech/social-gadgets/article/2150528/most-popular-iphone-app-tik-tok-hits-150-million-daily-users

73. Zhang, A. (June 13, 2018). Douyin Reveals User Numbers for the First Time. Retrieved October 18, 2018, from https://pandaily.com/douyin-reveals-user-numbers-for-the-first-time/

74. Jing, M. (May 10, 2018). Tencent-backed video app Kuaishou in overseas push amid increased China scrutiny. Retrieved October 8, 2018, from https://www.scmp.com/tech/china-tech/article/2145375/tencent-backed-video-app-kuaishou-overseas-push-amid-increased-china

75. Zhang, B. (December 22, 2017). The Performers Behind China's Much-Derided Livestreaming App. Retrieved September 19, 2018, from http://www.sixthtone.com/news/1001437/the-performers-behind-chinas-much-derided-livestreaming-ap

76. Jing, M. (April 2, 2018). Chinese live-streaming app Kuaishou cracks down on teenage mum videos following state media criticism. Retrieved October 8, 2018, from https://www.scmp.com/tech/start-ups/article/2139874/chinese-live-streaming-app-kuaishou-cracks-down-teenage-mom-videos

77.   Fan, F. (May 29, 2018). Short video mobile apps on the rise. Retrieved
      October 13, 2018, from http://www.chinadaily.com.cn/a/201805/29/
      WS5b0c9a68a31001b82571cc97.html

78.   Minter, A. (December 28, 2017). Chinese Populism Lives in a Video App. Retrieved
      September 23, 2018, from https://www.bloomberg.com/view/articles/2017-12-27/
      chinese-populism-lives-in-a-video-app

79.   Jing Travel. (May 15, 2018). Digital Deep Dive: How Mafengwo Drives Travel With
      User-generated Content. Retrieved September 23, 2018, from https://jingtravel.com/
      platform-deep-dive-series-mafengwo/

80.   Ruan, L. (April 24, 2017). From Modish Vane to Lawrence Li: These Are the Fashion
      Bloggers Shaping China's Luxury Industry (Part 2). Retrieved October 19, 2018, from
      https://jingdaily.com/modish-vane-lawrence-li-fashion-bloggers-shaping-chinas-
      luxury-industry-part-2/

81.   Ruan, L. (April 10, 2017). From Gogoboi to Mr. Bags: These Are the Fashion Bloggers
      Shaping China's Luxury Industry (Part 1). Retrieved October 19, 2018, from https://
      jingdaily.com/fashion-bloggers-shaping-chinas-luxury/

82.   Lee, E. (October 9, 2016). Six Well-funded Chinese "We-media" Startups Other Than
      Papi Jiang. Retrieved September 29, 2018, from https://technode.com/2016/10/09/
      we-media-papi-jiang/

83.   Hallanan, L. (January 26, 2018). Fatal Influencer Marketing Problems Start at
      the Campaign Brief. Retrieved October 9, 2018, from https://www.parklu.com/
      influencer-marketing-problems-campaign-brief/

84.   Hallanan, L. (June 8, 2018). Search Engine Optimization in China Utilizing a KOL
      Strategy. Retrieved September 4, 2018, from https://www.parklu.com/search-engine-
      optimization-china-kol-strategy/

85.   Hallanan, L. (April 12, 2018). Why Build Long-term Relationships with Influencers?.
      Retrieved September 4, 2018, from https://www.parklu.com/long-term-relationships-
      influencers/

86.   Hallanan, L. (April 26, 2018). CIM Episode 022: What Chinese Millennials Really
      Think About Social Media and Influencers With NYU Masters Students Jingyi Hu and
      Qianni An. Retrieved October 14, 2018, from http://www.chinainfluencermarketing.
      com/2018/04/cim022/

87.   Udemans, C. (July 5, 2018). Douyin to outsource KOL management to multi-channel
      networks. Retrieved September 28, 2018, from https://technode.com/2018/07/05/
      douyin-mcn/

88. Mediakix. (July 30, 2018). 6 Reasons Influencers Should Think Twice Before Joining A Youtube Network. Retrieved September 15, 2018, from http://mediakix.com/2018/07/youtube-network-mcn-benefits-disadvantages/#gs.XjBQTzQ

89. Hallanan, L. (March 28, 2018). CIM Episode 019: The Dark Arts of Chinese Agencies and a Plea for Brands to Stop Using Only the Top 1% of Influencers with Elijah Whaley. Retrieved October 15, 2018, from http://www.chinainfluencermarketing.com/2018/03/cim019/

90. Long, D. (February 19, 2018). Weibo passes the $1bn mark in revenues as the social networking site posts. Retrieved October 3, 2018, from https://www.thedrum.com/news/2018/02/19/weibo-passes-the-1bn-mark-revenues-the-social-networking-site-posts-strong-growth

91. Hallanan, L. (August 18, 2018). Total Guide to KOL Media Posts & Paid Weibo Advertising. Retrieved September 3, 2018, from https://www.parklu.com/kol-media-posts-paid-weibo-advertising/

92. Hallanan, L. (March 10, 2018). New Chinese Social Media Platforms' Rules Raise KOL Marketing Costs. Retrieved September 3, 2018, from https://www.parklu.com/chinese-social-media-platforms-kol-marketing/

93. Whaley, E. (November 2, 2017). Weibo and WeChat KOL Marketing Costs. Retrieved September 19, 2018, from https://www.parklu.com/weibo-wechat-kol-marketing-costs/

94. Hallanan, L. (May 2, 2018). Are Your Influencer Agency's Corrupt Practices Costing You? Retrieved September 26, 2018, from https://jingdaily.com/influencer-agency-corrupt/

95. Zheng, R. (February 20, 2018). China's "Water Army" Far Outnumbers US-Manufactured Followers. Retrieved October 17, 2018, from https://jingdaily.com/the-follower-factory-in-china/

96. Hallanan, L. (September 14, 2017). Ruhan: Blogger Incubators Disrupt China's Ecommerce Industry. Retrieved October 7, 2018, from https://www.parklu.com/ruhan-blogger-incubators-china-ecommerce/

97. Hallanan, L. (August 9, 2018). Micro KOL Marketing in China: What Brands Need to Know. Retrieved October 12, 2018, from https://www.parklu.com/micro-kol-marketing-china/

98. Hallanan, L. (May 14, 2018). Redbook Is a Vital Part of Any Beauty Brand's Marketing Mix. Retrieved October 15, 2018, from https://jingdaily.com/redbook-beauty-brands/

99. Evans, S. (February 10, 2018). The C-Suite: Gil Eyal, Founder of HYPR. Retrieved September 15, 2018, from https://www.brandingmag.com/2018/02/10/the-c-suite-gil-eyal-founder-of-hypr/

100. CBNData. (June 18, 2018). 90后、95后线上消费大数据洞察：青年养生派上线、吸猫吸狗成主流   Online consumption data insights for Post 90s and 95s. Retrieved October 21, 2018, from https://36kr.com/p/5139023.html

101. Hallanan, L. (December 29, 2017). Wechat Mini-Programs Revolutionize KOL Sales Campaigns. Retrieved September 5, 2018, from https://www.parklu.com/wechat-mini-programs-kol-sales-campaigns/

102. WalktheChat staff. (September 16, 2018). Is Weibo dead, or is it booming? Retrieved October 21, 2018, from https://mp.weixin.qq.com/s/QWO8kWPX0FekCmcTYwFmgw

103. Shankman, S. (May 17, 2018). The Rise of Live-streaming for Travel Marketing in China. Retrieved September 25, 2018, from https://jingtravel.com/the-rise-of-live-streaming-for-travel-marketing-in-china/

104. Hallanan, L. (June 21, 2017). Weitao KOLs Reinvent Taobao & Tmall Social Commerce. Retrieved September 17, 2018, from https://www.parklu.com/category/china-social-networks/weitao/

105. The Guardian. (July 20, 2007). Chinese actor writes world's top blog. Retrieved October 8, 2018, from https://www.theguardian.com/technology/2007/jul/20/news.newmedia

106. Willis, P. (July 23, 2007). Actress becomes world's favourite blogger. Retrieved October 18, 2018, from https://www.telegraph.co.uk/news/uknews/1558269/Actress-becomes-worlds-favourite-blogger.html

107. Hille, K. (January 14, 2010). Daring blogger tests the limits. Retrieved September 20, 2018, from https://www.webcitation.org/5moTqBOrK?url=http://www.ft.com/cms/s/0/ce3a018e-0126-11df-8c54-00144feabdc0.html?nclick_check=1

108. Martinsen, J. (September 26, 2008). Han Han seizes blogging crown from Xu Jinglei. Retrieved September 2, 2018, from http://www.danwei.org/blogs/han_han_seizes_the_blogging_cr.php

109. Buruma, I. (September 2, 2016). Essays by Han Han, the Chinese Blogger and Media Superstar. Retrieved September 27, 2018, from https://www.nytimes.com/2016/09/04/books/review/han-han-problem-with-me.html

110. South China Morning Post. (February 11, 2018). The 10 most influential fashion stylists in China. Retrieved September 27, 2018, from https://www.scmp.com/magazines/style/fashion-beauty/article/2132740/10-most-influential-fashion-stylists-china

111. Mike Golden. (September 9, 2018) China marketing and promotion through WeChat Key Opinion Leaders - the platform, and the law, is not on your side. Retrieved October 22, 2018, from http://blog.brandigo.com/brandigo-china-thinking/china-marketing-and-promotion-through-wechat-key-opinion-leaders-the-platform-and-the-law-is-not-on-your-side

112. Queennie Yang. (August 31, 2018) Meet The Chinese Influencers Making Waves In The Fashion World. Retrieved October 22, 2018, from   https://www.vogue.co.uk/article/chinese-influencers-to-know-now

113. Pan, Y. (January 26, 2018). The 8 Most Powerful Beauty Bloggers in China. Retrieved September 17, 2018, from https://jingdaily.com/chinese-beauty-kols-brands-need-to-know/

114. Dudarenok, A. (n.d.). How to launch your product on China's popular Xiaohongshu fashion platform. Retrieved October 17, 2018, from https://chozan.co/2018/07/25/launch-product-chinas-popular-xiaohongshu-fashion-platform/

115. Liz, F. (December 15, 2016). Jaeger LeCoultre Taps Online Celebrity Papi Jiang in Bid to Reach Chinese Millennials. Retrieved October 11, 2018, from https://jingdaily.com/jaeger-lecoultre-turns-to-outspoken-video-blogger-papi-jiang-in-bid-to-reach-chinese-millennials/

116. Graziani, T. (December 15, 2016). 6 Examples of Successful Douyin Marketing Campaigns. Retrieved October 2, 2018, from https://walkthechat.com/6-examples-successful-douyin-marketing-campaigns/

117. Today's ADTODAY. (May 9 2017). 百雀羚这幅广告把民国风做到了极致 This advertisement shows the ultimate Republic of China the ultimate. Retrieved October 11, 2018, from https://mp.weixin.qq.com/s/-vA5qils_oH6P7wbzR-5Ow

118. Sina. (May 23, 2018). 攻略分享带动用户活跃，旅游新零售运营新花样 | 2018年最新综合度假旅游预订应用TOP5 Retrieved October 22, 2018, from https://t.cj.sina.com.cn/articles/view/1716314577/664ce1d1019007j7d

119. Edited by Adam Bao, Transcribed by Frank Huang. (September 14, 2017). Short Video and Live-Streaming as a Platform – with Yixia Technology Divisional Head Spencer King. Retrieved October 22, 2018, from http://www.theharbingerchina.com/blog/short-video-and-live-streaming-as-a-platform-with-yixia-technology

120. Hongmei Li. (January 3, 2017). Advertising and Consumer Culture in China. Retrieved October 22, 2018, from https://www.chinacenter.net/2017/china_ currents/16-1/advertising-in-china/

121. Calfas, J. (July 5, 2018). A Ranking of the Richest Women of the Kardashian-Jenner Clan. Retrieved October 12, 2018, from http://time.com/money/4950313/kardashian-net-worth/

122. Lauren Hallanan. (November 9th, 2017). How to Use Live Streaming to Sell on China Ecommerce.   Retrieved October 22, 2018, from https://www.parklu.com/live-streaming-sell-china-ecommerce/

123. Jing Travel. (May 15, 2018). Digital Deep Dive: How Mafengwo Drives Travel With User-generated Content. Retrieved October 22, 2018, from https://jingtravel.com/ platform-deep-dive-series-mafengwo/

124. China Internet Watch. (August 8, 2018). Weibo monthly active users (MAU) grew to 431 million in Q2 2018. Retrieved October 22, 2018, from https://www. chinainternetwatch.com/26225/weibo-q2-2018/

125. Jiefei Liu. (July 17, 2018) Douyin reaches 500 million monthly active users worldwide. Retrieved October 22, 2018, from https://technode.com/2018/07/17/douyin-500-million-mau/

126. Alice Zhang. (June 13, 2018). Douyin Reveals User Numbers for the First Time. Retrieved October 22, 2018, from https://pandaily.com/douyin-reveals-user-numbers-for-the-first-time/

127. Meng Jing. (May 10, 2018). Tencent-backed video app Kuaishou in overseas push amid increased China scrutiny. Retrieved October 22, 2018, from https://www. scmp.com/tech/china-tech/article/2145375/tencent-backed-video-app-kuaishou-overseas-push-amid-increased-china

128. Emma Lee. (Aug 22, 2018). China's audio giant Ximalaya FM rumored to prepare for IPO. Retrieved October 22, 2018, from https://technode.com/2018/08/22/ximalaya-fm-ipo-rumor/

129. Fuyuan Hsiao. (May 5, 2017). Raking in NT$1.3B with Online Talkshow. Retrieved October 22, 2018, from https://english.cw.com.tw/article/article.action?id=1596

130. eMarketer Editors. (August 2, 2018). What's the Difference Between a KOL and a Wanghong? Savvy influencer marketers in China know. Retrieved October 21, 2018, from https://www.emarketer.com/content/what-s-the-difference-between-a-kol-and-a-wanghong

About the Authors

Ashley Dudarenok is a serial entrepreneur, professional speaker, vlogger, podcaster, media contributor and female entrepreneurship spokesperson. Her trademark expression is "Let's go get them," and she does. She's fluent in Mandarin, Russian, German and English. As a marketer and social media agency head with more than twelve years of professional experience in China and Hong Kong, she's seen the transformation of China's online world firsthand. Her specialties are China market entry, Chinese consumers, social media and the New Retail.

Ashley is the founder of multiple startups, including social media marketing agency Alarice and training enterprise ChoZan. Through Alarice, she and her team help clients from overseas make a splash on Chinese social media and help Chinese brands conquer western social media. Through ChoZan, which specializes in social media education and training, Ashley does corporate trainings, executive masterclasses and speaking engagements.

In 2017 alone she spoke at 58 events across Asia, Europe, and the Middle East. Ashley has appeared in Forbes, CNBC, the Huffington Post, the SCMP, TEDx and more. She's the host of the AshleyTalks Podcast, where she interviews top thought leaders from across Asia about entrepreneurship, China and tech.

Ashley loves to travel with her husband, box, play tennis and swim. She's fond of Shakespeare, live theater, watercolor painting and her dog.

Connect with Ashley on:
Linkedin.com/in/AshleyGalina
YouTube.com/c/AshleyTalksChina
Instagram.com/Ashley.Lina
Facebook.com/AshleyTalksChina
Twitter.com/AshleyDudarenok

Learn more at: ashleytalks.com, chozan.co or alarice.com.hk
Listen to the AshleyTalks podcast: www.ashleytalks.com/podcasts/
For speaking engagements or marketing training,
contact Ashley's team at ashley@chozan.co

Lauren Hallanan is the VP of Live Streaming at The Meet Group and a Chinese social media marketing expert focusing on influencer marketing, live streaming, and social commerce. She's a contributing writer at Forbes, Jing Daily, and PARKLU and host of the China Influencer Marketing and Stream Wars podcasts.

She herself is a China KOL, with followings on several Chinese social media platforms. On top of that she runs possibly the only website completely dedicated to analyzing the Chinese live streaming industry, www.chinalivestream.com, which she originally started as a way to document her journey of becoming a popular streamer with over 400,000 Chinese fans.

As host of the China Influencer Marketing Podcast she attempts to pull back the curtain on influencer marketing in China, speaking directly with top influencers, marketers and brands who share their experiences and reveal their strategies for success. In the Stream Wars podcast, she explores everything there is to know about the global live streaming industry, covering the latest trends from the top platforms both in China and the West.

She is available to speak, lead workshops, and consult on influencer marketing, live streaming, and social media marketing in China.

Outside of work, she's wife to the goofiest, tallest, most car-obsessed Chinese guy you'll ever meet, mom to an adorable stray dog that they found on the streets of China, a health nut and an outgoing introvert.

She previously lived in China for 8 years and is fluent in Mandarin. She's currently based in Upstate NY.

You can learn more and follow Lauren on the following platforms:
The China Influencer Marketing Podcast: www.chinainfluencermarketing.com
A collection of Lauren's articles: laurenhallanan.com/articles/
Chinese live streaming and social media trends: www.chinalivestream.com
Connect on LinkedIn: https://www.linkedin.com/in/lauren-hallanan/

First printing, 2018
ISBN 978-0-692-04190-1
2102, Iuki Tower,
5 O'Brien Road,
Wan Chai
Hong kong

Although the authors and publisher have made every effort to ensure that the information in this book was correct at press time, they do not assume and hereby disclaim any liability to any party for any loss, damage, or disruption caused by errors or omissions, whether such errors or omissions result from negligence, accident or any other cause.

The publisher has made every effort to ensure that URLs for external websites referred to in this book are correct and active at the time of going to press. However, the publisher has no responsibility for the websites and can make no guarantee that a site will remain live or that the content is or will remain appropriate.

Every effort has been made to trace all copyright holders but if any have been inadvertently overlooked, the publisher will be pleased to include any necessary credits in any subsequent reprint or edition.